INTRODUCING
ISSUES WITH
OPPOSING
VIEWPOINTS®

Prisons

Other books in the Introducing Issues
with Opposing Viewpoints series:

INTRODUCING
ISSUES WITH
OPPOSING
VIEWPOINTS®

Prisons

Lauri S. Friedman, *Book Editor*

Christine Nasso, *Publisher*
Elizabeth Des Chenes, *Managing Editor*

GREENHAVEN PRESS
An imprint of Thomson Gale, a part of The Thomson Corporation

THOMSON
GALE

Detroit • New York • San Francisco • New Haven, Conn. • Waterville, Maine • London

For more information, contact
Greenhaven Press
27500 Drake Rd.
Farmington Hills, MI 48331-3535
Or you can visit our Internet site at http://www.gale.com

LIBRARY OF CONGRESS CATALOGING-IN-PUBLICATION DATA

Prisons / Lauri S. Friedman, book editor.
     p. cm. — (Introducing issues with opposing viewpoints)
     Includes bibliographical references and index.
     ISBN-13: 978-0-7377-3578-9 (hardcover)
     1. Prisons—United States.   2. Prisoners—United States.   3. Imprisonment—United States.   4. Prisoners of war—United States.   I. Friedman, Lauri S.
     HV9471.P7826 2007
     365'.973—dc22

                                                                                    2007032513

ISBN-10: 0-7377-3578-3 (hardcover)

Printed in the United States of America

Contents

Foreword

Indulging in a wide spectrum of ideas, beliefs, and perspectives is a critical cornerstone of democracy. After all, it is often debates over differences of opinion, such as whether to legalize abortion, how to treat prisoners, or when to enact the death penalty that shape our society and drive it forward. Such diversity of thought is frequently regarded as the hallmark of a healthy and civilized culture. As the Reverend Clifford Schutjer of the First Congregational Church in Mansfield, Ohio, declared in a 2001 sermon, "Surrounding oneself with only like-minded people, restricting what we listen to or read only to what we find agreeable is irresponsible. Refusing to entertain doubts once we make up our minds is a subtle but deadly form of arrogance." With this advice in mind, Introducing Issues with Opposing Viewpoints books aim to open readers' minds to the critically divergent views that comprise our world's most important debates.

Introducing Issues with Opposing Viewpoints simplifies for students the enormous and often overwhelming mass of material now available via print and electronic media. Collected in every volume is an array of opinions that capture the essence of a particular controversy or topic. Introducing Issues with Opposing Viewpoints books embody the spirit of nineteenth-century journalist Charles A. Dana's axiom: "Fight for your opinions, but do not believe that they contain the whole truth, or the only truth." Absorbing such contrasting opinions teaches students to analyze the strength of an argument and compare it to its opposition. From this process readers can inform and strengthen their own opinions, or be exposed to new information that will change their minds. Introducing Issues with Opposing Viewpoints is a mosaic of different voices. The authors are statesmen, pundits, academics, journalists, corporations, and ordinary people who have felt compelled to share their experiences and ideas in a public forum. Their words have been collected from newspapers, journals, books, speeches, interviews, and the Internet, the fastest growing body of opinionated material in the world.

Introducing Issues with Opposing Viewpoints shares many of the well-known features of its critically acclaimed parent series, Opposing Viewpoints. The articles are presented in a pro/con format, allowing readers to absorb divergent perspectives side by side. Active reading questions preface each viewpoint, requiring the student to approach the material thoughtfully and carefully. Useful charts, graphs, and cartoons supplement each article. A thorough introduction provides readers with crucial background on an issue. An annotated bibliography points the reader toward articles, books, and Web sites that contain additional information on the topic. An appendix of organizations to contact contains a wide variety of charities, nonprofit organizations, political groups, and private enterprises that each hold a position on the issue at hand. Finally, a comprehensive index allows readers to locate content quickly and efficiently.

Introducing Issues with Opposing Viewpoints is also significantly different from Opposing Viewpoints. As the series title implies, its presentation will help introduce students to the concept of opposing viewpoints, and learn to use this material to aid in critical writing and debate. The series' four-color, accessible format makes the books attractive and inviting to readers of all levels. In addition, each viewpoint has been carefully edited to maximize a reader's understanding of the content. Short but thorough viewpoints capture the essence of an argument. A substantial, thought-provoking essay question placed at the end of each viewpoint asks the student to further investigate the issues raised in the viewpoint, compare and contrast two authors' arguments, or consider how one might go about forming an opinion on the topic at hand. Each viewpoint contains sidebars that include at-a-glance information and handy statistics. A Facts About section located in the back of the book further supplies students with relevant facts and figures.

Following in the tradition of the Opposing Viewpoints series, Greenhaven Press continues to provide readers with invaluable exposure to the controversial issues that shape our world. As John Stuart Mill once wrote: "The only way in which a human being can make some approach to knowing the whole of a subject is by hearing what can be said about it by persons of every variety of opinion and studying all modes in which it can be looked at by every character of mind. No wise man ever acquired his wisdom in any mode but this." It is to this principle that Introducing Issues with Opposing Viewpoints books are dedicated.

Introduction

When people study the issues relating to prisons and inmates, a consistent and recurring theme is how prisoners should be treated. It is widely agreed that it is important to treat prisoners humanely because this reflects positively on the incarcerating society. Furthermore, good treatment can help rehabilitate prisoners and, in case someone has been incarcerated mistakenly, it prevents that person from being unduly abused. But because prisoners have broken the law and in doing so have mistreated or even murdered others, it is also argued that their treatment should reflect the fact that they are being punished for unacceptable—and at times horrific—crimes.

The issue of how to treat prisoners was thrust into the spotlight in an especially complicated way after the U.S. government began capturing prisoners in the war on terror. In addition to the need for a place to house these prisoners, it was unclear initially what to call them. In past wars, enemy fighters who were captured were labeled "prisoners of war," and as thus were afforded certain protections under the Geneva Conventions. (The Geneva Conventions were widely adopted after World War II and for more than half a century have been regarded as a comprehensive guide for undertaking global conflict.)

Today's war on terror, however, involves actors not explicitly mentioned in the Geneva Conventions, which were intended to cover traditional wars between nation-states. The Geneva Conventions define prisoners of war as soldiers, meaning those who wear the uniform of their nation, have a rank and a superior, fight openly, and avoid violence against civilians. The term "prisoners of war," therefore, did not seem to apply to "soldiers" who fought not under a national army but on behalf of a terrorist group. Instead, American leaders determined a more appropriate term for the prisoners was "enemy combatants" or "unlawful combatants". Though this label did not afford them the protections under the Geneva Conventions, it was promised that the combatants would be treated humanely. They were moved to a U.S. naval base at Guantanamo Bay, Cuba, where some have remained for more than five years.

Almost immediately after the first inmate arrived in Cuba, controversy began to swirl around the way the inmates were treated. Reports abounded that severe abuses and human rights violations were taking place, such as the torture and humiliation of inmates by American guards. One prisoner was reportedly forced to strip naked, bark like a dog, wear pictures of near-naked women around his neck, and forced to go to the bathroom in his pants. His and other experiences have been well documented by Amnesty International, the Red Cross, Human Rights Watch, and other international organizations. For this reason, writer Bill Press has described Guantanamo Bay as "the big black eye on the face of the United States, contradicting everything we supposedly stand for—in terms of human rights, human decency, and respect for the law. No wonder Amnesty International has branded it 'the gulag of our times.'"

Many argue that in addition to physical mistreatment, the prolonged detainment is a form of torture and mistreatment itself. Indeed, most of the enemy combatants have been incarcerated at Guantanamo Bay since the 2001 War in Afghanistan. As of November 2006, according to MSNBC, just 340 of the original 775 detainees had been released. Of the remaining 435,110 have been labeled as ready for release, and the remaining 325 will either face trial or continue to be held indefinitely. Many argue that this type of detention is a blatant violation of both international and U.S. law. Says attorney Michael Ratner, "It's shocking to anyone who believes in the rule of law. Indefinite detention without any legitimate court process is unheard of in this country."

Yet other reports state that the Guantanamo Bay detainees have been treated well and in accordance with both international and domestic law. According to one BBC report, upon arrival each prisoner was given a foam sleeping mat, a blanket, two buckets, a canteen, two jumpsuits, a pair of flip-flops, two towels, a washcloth, toothpaste, soap, shampoo, and a copy of the Koran. All meals served at Guantanamo have been deemed "culturally appropriate," meaning they do not violate any Muslim dietary restrictions. Guantanamo inmates are served three meals a day. For breakfast, they are typically served bread, cream cheese, an orange, a pastry, a roll, and water. Lunch consists of a box of cereal, two cereal bars, a packet of peanuts, potato chips, raisins, and water. A typical dinner consists of white rice, red beans, a banana, bread, and water. As for the inmates' routines, they are allowed two opportunities to shower each day, are granted a daily exercise period, and are allowed time to write letters using pens and paper that are provided during a supervised letter writing time. "If this is unacceptable, 'gulag' style 'torture,' then every inmate in America is a victim of human-rights violations," writes columnist Michelle Malkin, who believes reports of abuse at Guantanamo Bay have been exaggerated.

Furthermore, some argue that even if unlawful combatants were to be mistreated at Guantanamo Bay, this is the price they pay for having perpetrated attacks against Americans. As author Tammy Bruce puts it, "When it comes to al-Qaeda leadership and operatives, anything goes. I don't care if you put women's underwear on their heads, or frankly, even pull out a few fingernails of those responsible for mass murder, to unmask their continuing plans for the genocide of civilized peoples . . . It's called 'torture lite,' it works, and I'm all for whatever it takes to get information, and yes, to punish and annihilate terrorist leadership around the world." Bruce and others argue it is not fair to hold the United States to high international standards while fighting an enemy that would willingly punch below the belt to kill innocent Americans.

Examining the treatment of prisoners in the context of the war on terror is one of many issues explored in Introducing Issues with Opposing Viewpoints: Prisons. Readers will also consider arguments about whether prisons help or hurt society, whether they reduce crime, whether they effectively reform inmates, and whether inmates are treated humanely. The wealth of information and perspectives provided in the article pairs will help students come to their own conclusions about how prisoners should be treated and whether prisons get America further from, or closer to, being a crime-free society.

Chapter 1

Do Prisons Help Society?

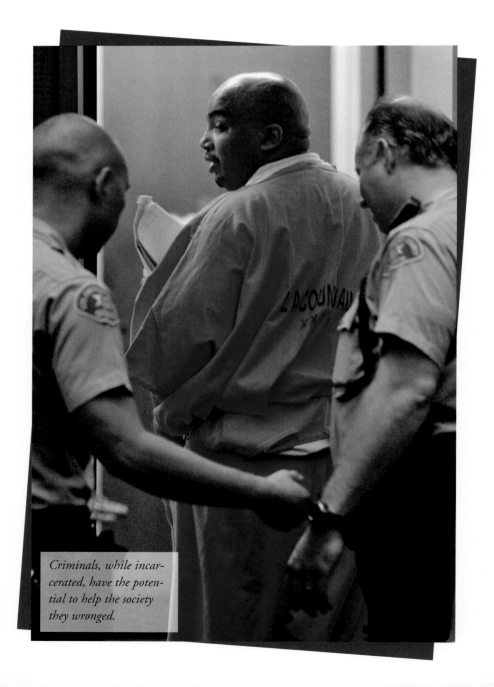

Criminals, while incarcerated, have the potential to help the society they wronged.

Prisons Are Beneficial to Society

David Muhlhausen

"America does not love prisons. We'd far rather neither have nor need them. But some of us clearly need to be in prison for the safety of the rest of us."

In the following viewpoint, author David Muhlhausen argues that the United States needs prisons to keep its citizenry safe. He laments recent trends that harsh prison sentences have been replaced by rehabilitation programs, probation, or slap-on-the-wrist sentences. When criminals are treated leniently, he explains, there are more criminals on the streets. This not only puts more Americans at risk from crime, rape, and murder, but sends the message to would-be criminals that crime is not seriously punished. For these reasons, Muhlhausen concludes that America must abandon its lenient sentencing laws and reinvest in prisons.

David Muhlhausen is a senior research analyst in the Center for Data Analysis at the Heritage Foundation, a research and educational institute that published this viewpoint.

AS YOU READ, CONSIDER THE FOLLOWING QUESTIONS:
  1. How much has the prison population grown since 1980, according to the author?

Signs can be found nationwide that what critics call America's "love affair" with incarcerating prisoners may be coming to an end.

Extending Leniency to Those Who Don't Deserve It

The legislature of Washington state, which passed the nation's first three-strikes-you're-out law by popular initiative a decade ago, recently passed a series of laws weakening it. Kansas now orders first-time drug offenders to treatment rather than prison, provided they didn't commit a crime that involved violence. Michigan has dropped its lengthy mandatory-minimum sentences for drug offenders. Iowa, Missouri and Wisconsin have eased their "truth in sentencing" laws, which require inmates to serve nearly their entire sentences before being eligible for parole.

FAST FACT

As of 2004, 1 of every 138 Americans was incarcerated in prison or jail.

In the last year, 25 states have sought to reduce the burden on their budgets and their corrections systems by weakening mandatory-sentencing statutes, reforming post-release requirements and restoring parole. Those proposing these measures come from both sides of the political aisle and from every level of government. They include sheriffs and police chiefs, legislators and members of Congress, governors and prison executives.

But if Alan Elsner, an author who focuses on criminal-justice issues, was correct in a recent op-ed for the *Washington Post* that our "love affair" with incarcerating dangerous criminals is waning, those proposing the changes are going to find that breaking up is hard to do. Americans have come to rely on the criminal-justice system to keep hard-core offenders locked up, and they won't think it's worth it when—in the name of cost-cutting—rapes, murders and other violent crimes go up by the thousands as a result of any veiled efforts to extend leniency to offenders who clearly don't deserve it.

It Pays to Lock Up Criminals

The American people understand their state governments are in financial crisis and that the federal government expects record deficits in the near future. They sense that locking up some prisoners—first-time drug offenders, for instance—may be draining state money needlessly. The increased emphasis on rehabilitating prisoners and easing their return to society that President Bush advocated in his recent State of the Union speech makes sense to many of them.

But they also know that the strengthening of sentencing laws in the early 1990s, the prison-building boom that began in that decade and efforts by prosecutors and lawmakers to take dangerous criminals off the street and keep them off has paid handsome dividends.

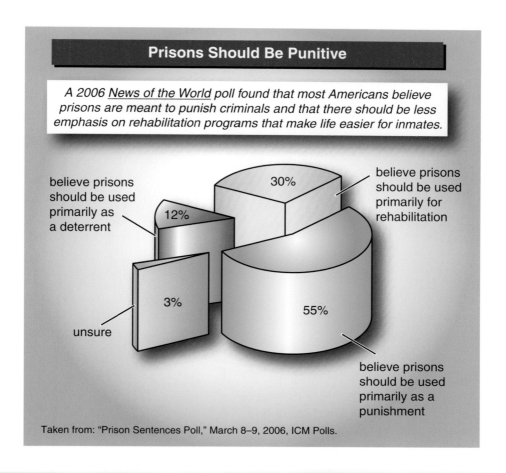

Prisons Should Be Punitive

A 2006 *News of the World* poll found that most Americans believe prisons are meant to punish criminals and that there should be less emphasis on rehabilitation programs that make life easier for inmates.

believe prisons should be used primarily as a deterrent

12%

30%

believe prisons should be used primarily for rehabilitation

3%

unsure

55%

believe prisons should be used primarily as a punishment

Taken from: "Prison Sentences Poll," March 8–9, 2006, ICM Polls.

Prisons Keep Americans Safe

The prison population in America has quadruped since 1980 to more than 2 million people. Crime rates during the decade dropped to all-time lows. Coincidence? Consider that researchers have found that 15 crimes are committed for every person released from prison, and

Society has seen rapid prison reform programs rehabilitate felons and reintroduce them to society.

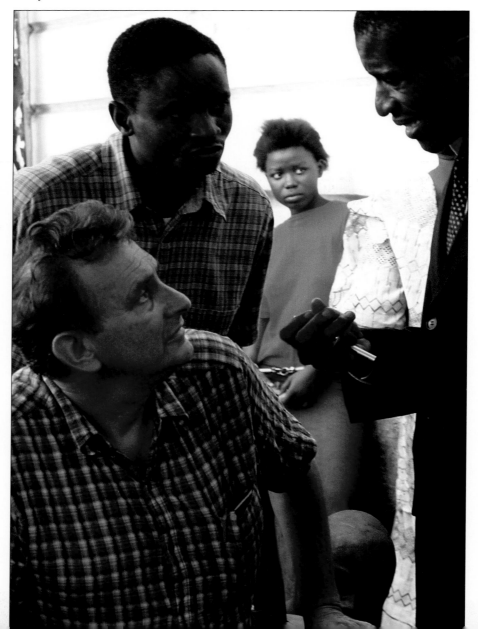

that 17 crimes are avoided for every person put into prison. Also along those lines, a 10 percent increase in prison population leads to a 13 percent decrease in homicides.

Considering that half the people in America's prisons are serving time for violent crimes, that means that, conservatively, millions of people have avoided becoming victims of such crimes thanks to these policies. So pardon them if they're not quick to slash corrections budgets when corrections makes up so small a part of states' operational expenditures—about 6.7 percent, according to the latest research. Pardon their skepticism of a rehabilitation system with a long, miserable record of failure—two-thirds of those released from prison this year will be re-arrested within three years and almost 49 percent of the violent criminals released will return to prison in that time period.

Finding Room In the Budget

There is a lot of discussion in the country these days about the proper role and size of government. But all agree that providing for the public safety is its first and foremost job.

Right now, that means operating and building prisons will remain for some time to come a significant priority of government. America's state prisons operate today at up to 117 percent capacity, which means two things: we must ensure we incarcerate only those who truly should be in prison, and we must face the fact that we need more prisons, not fewer.

States can save money by more effectively prioritizing within their criminal-justice systems. They can find alternatives for first-time drug offenders and others who haven't committed violent crimes. They can bolster vocational training, which shows some promise of better preparing prisoners to find employment after release.

We Need Prisons

But there's only so much that can be done. America faced a real problem when the prison-building and sentence-strengthening movements began—a wave of violent crime that left much of the nation gripped in fear. This problem got better in the 1990s, but it hasn't gone away. And even if we can decrease recidivism, those who commit crimes, especially violent crimes, owe a debt to society and need to do their time. In truth, America does not love prisons. We'd far rather neither have nor need them. But some of us clearly need to be in prison for the safety of the rest of us. As long as that's the case, we can, will and, indeed, must spend the money to do what it takes to incarcerate those people. Which means that breaking up with the tough law enforcement of the 1990s will be indeed be hard to do.

EVALUATING THE AUTHOR'S ARGUMENTS:

David Muhlhausen uses statistics, anecdotes and reason to make his argument, but does not include any quotations to support his position. List three types of voices Muhlhausen could have quoted from to strengthen his argument, and what these voices might have said.

Prisons are Not Beneficial to Society

Jeffrey Ian Ross

"Prisons are . . . meant to rehabilitate criminals and to keep them from victimizing others in the future. But they rarely succeed at that goal."

In the following viewpoint, author Jeffrey Ian Ross argues that prisons have failed to rehabilitate criminals, and serve only to increase violence in America. Ross paints a picture of violent, dirty, and chaotic prisons in which inmates, instead of learning from their past mistakes, only become further hardened to violence and crime. Furthermore, many inmates imprisoned for nonviolent crimes such as drug arrests learn to be violent in prison, says Ross. He urges Americans to rethink their prison system, arguing the emphasis of incarceration should be on education and rehabilitation rather than on punishment and restriction. Jeffrey Ian Ross is a fellow with the Center for Comparative and International Law, University of Baltimore. He is the author, coauthor, editor, and coeditor of eleven books, including *Behind Bars: Surviving Prison, Convict Criminology,* and *Special Problems in Corrections*. Ross worked for almost four years in a correctional facility.

AS YOU READ, CONSIDER THE FOLLOWING QUESTIONS:
1. What diseases are prisoners prone to, and how does this affect their ability to be rehabilitated, according to Ross?
2. According to the author, how many people were incarcerated in America in 2004?
3. What does the word "recidivism" mean in the context of the viewpoint?

Keith DeBlasio was 28 when he was sentenced to five years in federal prison for passing $200,000 in forged cashiers' checks across state lines. He had never committed a violent crime. During his first two months of incarceration, he was repeatedly raped, and his cellmate threatened to stab him. He is now HIV positive. A similar fate befell Garrett Cunningham in 2000. While incarcerated at the Luther Unit of the Texas Department of Criminal Justice, he was repeatedly raped by a correctional officer.

American jails and prisons don't work.

Prisons Increase Violence

Prisons are meant to protect the community, but incarcerating people has minimal effect on the crime rate. Violent offenders are released to make way for nonviolent first time offenders, and most people, if they survive the prison experience, are worse off when they get out. About two-thirds of all inmates released from prisons are rearrested within three years.

Prisons are meant to punish those who have committed a crime, but usually do so with excessive and unintended cruelty. Violence, including sexual assault, is rampant. The unsanitary living conditions, combined with the absence of adequate health and medical care, mean that prison inmates and workers are highly susceptible to life-threatening diseases like AIDS, hepatitis, TB and food poisoning. These problems frustrate inmates and often lead to anger, depression and more violence.

Perhaps more importantly, prisons are also meant to rehabilitate criminals and to keep them from victimizing others in the future. But they rarely succeed at that goal. Meaningful vocational and educational programs are rarely offered. And if they are, prisoners practically have to run an obstacle course in order to get access to or complete the classes.

A Problematic Prison Boom

And yet, despite the failure of our correctional facilities, we're sending more people to them than ever. Over the past two decades, as a result of harsher sentencing laws and the war on drugs, America has experienced one of the largest expansions in its jail, prison and community corrections populations in history. In 2004, according to Department of Justice, approximately 2.1 million people were in jails or prisons, and 4.9 million more were in some form of community corrections (typically probation or parole). That is roughly 3.5% of the adult population. Unsurprisingly, America leads the world in the number of people it incarcerates per capita.

That is why, short of abolishing prisons, which is not as radical as it sounds, we need to examine how correctional facilities in America can be reinvented.

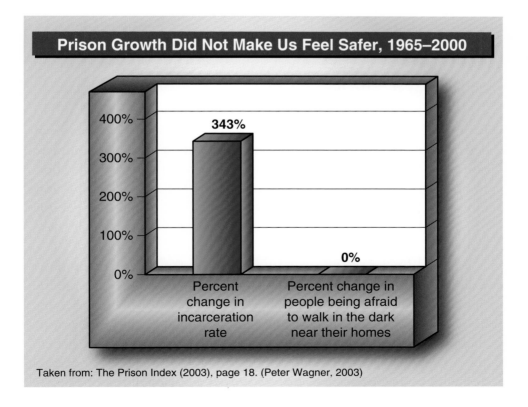

Prison Growth Did Not Make Us Feel Safer, 1965–2000

Taken from: The Prison Index (2003), page 18. (Peter Wagner, 2003)

Prisoners are not always enrolled in rehabilitation programs, and many believe this is why prisons are not beneficial.

Changing the Purpose of Prison

To begin with, the federal government should implement a "No Prisoner Left Behind" program, which requires state correctional departments to insure that all prisoners pass their GEDs and complete one or more technical training courses. Moreover, university education should be facilitated for any prisoner upon request. We know that most inmates have no marketable skills to rely on when they get out of jail or prison. It is incumbent on the system to ensure that these individuals have at least a high school education.

We can also reduce prison populations by transferring many non-violent inmates to community corrections programs. Traditionally, this has meant probation or parole. But, more recently, these programs have also come to rely on electronic monitoring devices, house arrest, chemical castration and intensive supervision, all of which have generally proven to keep inmates in check. In December 2003, in order to deal with budget deficits, Kentucky started releasing numerous short-timers (those with less than a year on their sentence) who had been convicted of nonviolent crimes. This action had minimal effect on recidivism rates.

From Punishment to Reward

Once the jail and prison populations come down to a manageable size, correctional officers should

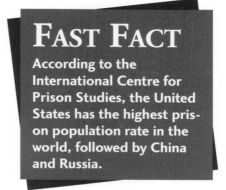

be encouraged, through educational and salary incentives, to switch from their current roles—in which they basically function like hotel attendants—to becoming true "Rehabilitation Officers," implementing and managing meaningful rehabilitation programs.

Prison systems should be rewarded for their ability to rehabilitate inmates, not for simply preventing inmates from escaping. State corrections departments should be given more money if their released inmates prove to commit fewer crimes.

Making Prisons More Effective

Of course, it must be understood that some individuals will never be appropriate for release into society. These people must be housed in secure facilities. But jails and prisons should really be reserved only for the most violent criminals.

They should be smaller, too. Large correctional facilities are costly to run, unnecessarily bureaucratic and impersonal. Smaller physical structures go a long way in minimizing the alienation of prisoners and correctional officers alike. The older facilities can be torn down, used as homeless shelters, or as tourist attractions for the public to see the way that we used to do things.

Within the remaining prisons and jails, we need to re-think the way prisoners are housed. Older, more experienced prisoners typically prey on younger prisoners. This leads to both physical and sexual violence. Over time, younger prisoners become socialized to prison life, making it more difficult for them to re-enter society. Violent prisoners who have committed felonies should never be mixed with first time offenders or people convicted of nonviolent crimes.

Fixing a Failed System

Over the past 200 years, American jails and prisons have adopted a fortress mentality. Wardens and correctional administrators should be more amenable to continuous inspection, and should even allow the public to take a regular look at what goes on behind bars. This should simultaneously serve as a deterrent against abuse of inmates, and to help "scare straight" juveniles at risk of a life of crime, providing them with a wake up call to mend their ways.

Until American jails and prisons are reinvented, the number of people wasting away behind the razor wire and high walls will continue to grow. They represent the worst of a failed system that foreigners constantly point to as a lack of American ingenuity.

EVALUATING THE AUTHOR'S ARGUMENTS:

The author chose to open his essay with the stories of Keith DeBlasio and Garrett Cunningham. What are their stories, and how do they serve to underscore the author's main argument? Did you find this to be an effective way to capture a reader's attention? Explain why or why not.

Prisons Keep Criminals off the Streets

Robert Whelan

"While we wish all the best to those who are work-ing to reform criminals, we look to the prisons to keep them out of harm's way. Our harm, that is."

In the following viewpoint, author Robert Whelan argues that prisons serve a very basic, and necessary, function: to keep criminals off the streets. Instead of expend-ing effort debating the usefulness of prisons, Whelan argues that more time should be spent incarcerating criminals: doubling Britain's prison population, according to the author, could prevent more than nine million crimes. The U.K. is already too lenient on locking up criminals, in his opinion, and innocent citizens pay for this mistake. Although alternatives to prison seem like a nice idea, Whelan argues none are as effective at reducing the crime rate as incarceration. Therefore, he concludes that society should support the use of prisons as the best way to keep crime rates low. Robert Whelan is the deputy director of Civitas, an independent think tank that seeks to deep-en public understanding of the legal, insti-tutional and moral framework that makes possible a free society.

AS YOU READ, CONSIDER THE FOLLOWING QUESTIONS:
1. According to the author, what is the average number of prisoners for every 1,000 recorded crimes?
2. What evidence does Whelan use as a reason to characterize the British as a "flabby, lefty liberal bunch of do-gooders"?
3. What does the word "stigmatized" mean in the context of the viewpoint?

S ome years ago, I was taken on a tour of the prison—now a centre for young offenders—to which [author] Oscar Wilde was sent in 1895. Wilde was an early campaigner against prisons and punishment. *The Ballad of Reading Gaol* is one of the most impor-

Even with overcrowded prison systems, the belief that jails keep criminals from running free is still standard.

tant, best written, anti-prison diatribes [a long, bitter discourse on the topic]. Its author viewed imprisonment as more cruel than the crimes that sent men there and an expression of the hypocrisy of a society which punished the powerless, while leaving influential malefactors [criminals] at large.

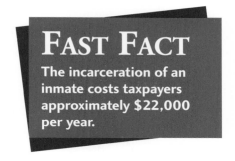

In Wilde's day, this view was the preserve of a few writers, social reformers and upper-class socialists. If he could come back today, he would be amazed at the way in which his sentiments have become the lingua franca [the most common form of communication] of the entire criminal justice system.

What point is there in sending people to prison, we are asked? It just makes them more professional criminals and leads to reoffending as soon as they are released. They are stigmatised and will never get back into mainstream society. Incarceration is so inhumane, it should have no place in a modern, caring society. We don't have to wait for gay poets, banged up for offences with rent boys, to dish out these truisms: we get them from lawyers, probation officers, social workers and even, in some particularly distressing cases, from judges.

The view that we are entitled to use prisons to indicate that certain forms of behaviour will not be tolerated, and to protect ourselves against people who refuse to play by the rules, has become the policy position that dare not speak its name. The strange thing is that the majority of the population holds that view. As ordinary people have no say over the way in which the criminal justice system is run, that is irrelevant.

We are constantly being berated by the crime professionals over the fact that Britain has the largest prison population—in terms of prisoners per thousand population—in Europe. This is meant to indicate that we are a vindictive society and that we should aim to have fewer prisoners. The view is put, unchallenged, over and over again, so it may seem paradoxical to point out that the size of the prison population may not reflect the vindictiveness of society: it may reflect the level of crime.

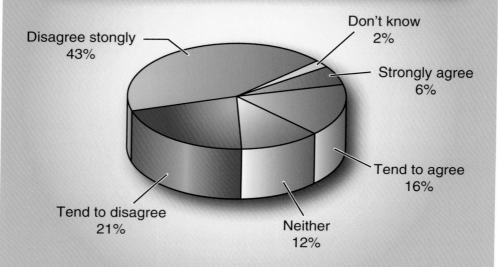

Prisons Keep Criminals off the Streets

A 2006 poll found that most Americans believe that keeping criminals in prison for longer benefits society. When asked whether the early release of prisoners is a good way of rehabilitating them back into the community, the majority disagreed.

Disagree stongly
43%

Don't know
2%

Strongly agree
6%

Tend to agree
16%

Neither
12%

Tend to disagree
21%

Taken from: "Prison Sentences Poll," March 8–9, 2006, *ICM Polls.*

The fact is that Britain is a particularly crime-ridden country. Levels of crime are staggeringly high here, both compared with our own historical situation and with other developed countries.

The more relevant statistic than the proportion of the population in prison would be the number of people we have in prison in relation to the number of crimes committed. On this measure, we come across as a flabby, lefty liberal bunch of do-gooders.

Across the EU [European Union], there are, on average, 17.7 prisoners for every 1,000 recorded crimes. We have 12.7, so we would need to increase our prison population by 50 per cent just to get it up to the European average. The Irish have 39.4 prisoners for every 1,000 recorded crimes, and the Spanish 49.1, so we would need to triple or quadruple the prison population to catch up with the supposedly more laid-back Latins and Celts.

And what an advantage that would be to the rest of us. The Home Office estimates that the average offender commits 140 offences in a year. If we were to double the prison population from 65,000 to 130,000, we would be protecting the public from more than nine million offences.

The advantages of such a policy are so obvious that it is difficult to think of a counter-argument. This makes no difference, because the criminal justice system is run by people who do not intend to consider the possibility.

If you were to raise the point at a gathering of these good people, you would be treated as if you had made a racist remark. People wouldn't attack you, they would just start talking across you.

As for the supposed advantages of the "alternatives to prison", we are still waiting for the evidence that they exist. Community sentencing, tagging, fines—how wonderful it would be if they worked, then we could allow criminals to walk the streets without apprehension.

Unfortunately, there is very little to be said for any of these alternatives. Although the criminal justice professionals believe passionately that they reduce reoffending rates, there is little evidence that they do any good.

Tagging [a criminal with a monitoring bracelet] is, in the Home Office's tactful phrase, "broadly neutral" in its effect on behaviour, ie, makes no difference. (The young thug called Slasher who nearly killed a woman in a London park was tagged.)

Probation does not reduce reoffending, compared with those sentenced to a combination of prison and probation, or community service. Some studies show higher reoffending rates for probationers. Fines are often not paid and little effort is put into chasing them. Cognitive behavioural therapy, in which this Government has invested so much, is so useless it should be scrapped.

"I am not at all in favour of this modern fashion for turning bad people into good people overnight," says one of Oscar Wilde's

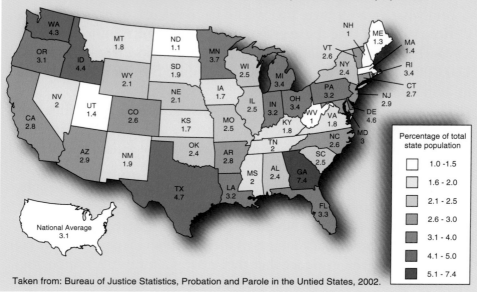

Texas, Washington, Idaho, and Georgia incarcerate the highest percentages of their population while others, such as West Virginia, New Hampshire, New Mexico, and Maine incarcerate fewer percent of the population

Percentage of total state population

☐	1.0 - 1.5
☐	1.6 - 2.0
☐	2.1 - 2.5
▨	2.6 - 3.0
▨	3.1 - 4.0
▨	4.1 - 5.0
■	5.1 - 7.4

National Average 3.1

Taken from: Bureau of Justice Statistics, Probation and Parole in the Untied States, 2002.

dowagers [a wealthy widow whose money comes from her deceased husband]. "As a man sows, so should he reap."

Well, she need have no worry. Prison doesn't make bad people good, and neither do the alternatives, in the majority of cases.

Of course, people can change. They may experience a religious conversion, conquer a drug habit or undergo a revolution in their lifestyle that changes their behaviour. Getting married is the best way out of crime for young men. But, in the meantime, while we wish all the best to those who are working to reform criminals, we look to the prisons to keep them out of harm's way. Our harm, that is.

EVALUATING THE AUTHOR'S ARGUMENTS:

1. Robert Whelan examines alternatives to prison, such as tagging, probation, and therapy, but concludes that none effectively curb crime as well as prisons. Explain why the author disapproves of each of these methods, and then state your own opinion on whether prisons are the best tool for reducing crime.
2. After reading Whelan's article, do you think he believes criminals can ever be successfully rehabilitated? Why or why not?

Viewpoint 4

Prisons Are Filled With People Who Don't Belong There

Jamie Fellner

"Prisons have become the nation's mental health facilities."

Prisons have become warehouses for the mentally ill, according to Jamie Fellner in the following viewpoint. Because the nation's mental health facilities are unequipped to handle the volume of people who need treatment, many mentally ill people who commit non-violent or minor crimes are shipped off to prison. Fellner explains that not only is this a misuse of prison facilities, but the mentally ill are uniquely disadvantaged in the prison environment. She urges states to refrain from locking up the mentally ill and to improve mental health facilities to properly help those who need treatment so they do not have to suffer incarceration.

Jamie Fellner is the director of the U.S. Program of Human Rights Watch, an organization that advocates alternatives to prison, among other human rights reforms.

Jamie Fellner, "Cruel and Sadly Usual: Prisons Shouldn't Be Mental Wards," *Boston Herald*, March 26, 2007. Reproduced by permission of the author.

AS YOU READ, CONSIDER THE FOLLOWING QUESTIONS:
1. According to Fellner, prisons house how many more mentally ill people than mental health hospitals?
2. How many mentally ill inmates are convicted of nonviolent offenses, as reported by Fellner?
3. List three ways in which the mentally ill are unable to handle the prison environment, according to the author.

Twelve years ago a federal judge ruled unconstitutional California's practice of putting mentally ill prisoners in solitary confinement. It is, he said, the equivalent of putting an "asthmatic in a room with no air." Since then, inmates have won settlements or court orders in at least seven states to keep prisoners with serious mental illness out of "solitary" or what corrections officials prefer to call segregation.

In Massachusetts, there will likely be a similar victory in the lawsuit filed [in 2007] against the Department of Corrections. The evidence is

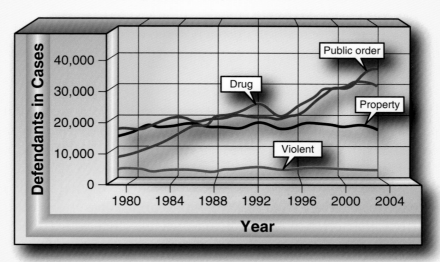

Prisons Are Not Filled with Violent Criminals

The majority of people in prison are incarcerated due to non-violent offenses, such as drug arrests and public order violations.

Taken from: Compendium of Federal Justice Statistics, annual.

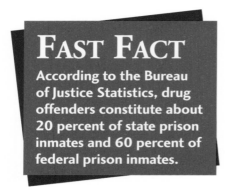

overwhelming that it is cruel and a violation of basic human dignity to force prisoners with serious mental illness to spend years confined round the clock in claustrophobic cells, with nothing to do, and no one with whom to have a normal conversation. The cruelty is compounded because mental health services for segregated prisoners typically consist of nothing more than medication and brief periodic cell-front checks-ins.

Prisons Have Become Mental Health Wards

Prisoners with serious mental illness need structured days and interaction with others. They need group therapy, individual counseling, training in daily living, education about their illness, supervised recreation and other forms of psychiatric rehabilitation as well as medication. Yet as is often the case in prison, security and punishment trump mental health needs.

Untreated or undertreated, the mentally ill in segregation may deteriorate. They may rant and rave, babble incoherently or huddle silently. They may talk to invisible friends and live in worlds constructed of hallucinations. They may beat their heads against walls, yell endlessly, cover themselves with feces and self-mutilate until their bodies are riddled with scars. Many try suicide; some succeed.

Why are there mentally ill prisoners in segregation? Because prisons have become the nation's mental health facilities.

In Prison for the Wrong Reasons

Prisons now house three times more people with serious mental illness such as schizophrenia, bipolar disorder and major depression than mental health hospitals. The federal Bureau of Justice Statistics says half of state prisoners nationwide have a mental health problem.

They end up in prison because the community mental health systems are in shambles—fragmented, underfunded and unable to serve the poor, the homeless and those who are substance-addicted as well as mentally ill.

As state mental hospitals become more scarce, regular prison populations are being forced to take those who would be considered mental patients who have committed crimes.

Nationwide, half of the state inmates with mental health problems were convicted of nonviolent offenses, primarily low-level drug and property offenses. Alternatives to incarceration may have been appropriate, but the court's hands are tied by mandatory sentencing laws.

An Unfair Punishment for Those Unable to Handle It

Once behind bars, the mentally ill find themselves ill-equipped to handle the stresses and rules—formal and informal—of prison life. They are more likely to be victimized and more likely to be injured in a fight than other inmates. They are more likely to break the rules. They are more likely to behave in ways that annoy, disgust and even enrage security staff who have scant training in how to recognize, much less cope with, symptoms of mental illness.

Moreover, prison mental health services across the country are woefully deficient, crippled by understaffing, insufficient facilities and limited programs, and swamped by the sheer number of prisoners who need them. Lacking resources and options, prison officials put problem prisoners, including the mentally ill, in segregation, where by virtue of being locked up around the clock they cause less trouble.

Let's Keep the Mentally Ill Out of Prison

States can institute policies to keep mentally ill inmates out of segregation or wait for litigation to force them to do so. They can improve the quantity and quality of mental health services they provide. But even those necessary steps fail to confront the larger question—should prisons be de facto mental institutions? If not, then the country must reduce the number of mentally ill people who are incarcerated.

The starting point is to reform needlessly harsh and counter-productive sentencing laws. States must also increase the scope and effectiveness of community mental health systems. The mentally ill do not have to end up in prison, but first elected officials must show far more compassion and common sense than they have to date.

EVALUATING THE AUTHOR'S ARGUMENTS:

In this viewpoint, Jamie Fellner describes prisons as mostly filled with mentally ill, nonviolent people who have committed minor offenses. In the previous viewpoint, Robert Whelan describes prisons as holding an overwhelming number of violent, dangerous criminals. After reading both viewpoints, which author's picture of prison do you think is more accurate? Explain your answer using evidence from the text.

Viewpoint

5

Faith-Based Prisons Are Beneficial to Society

Rob Moll

> *"We welcome them [ex-prisoners] back into society, particularly those who have been changed by Christ and need a church home, a Bible study group, a mentor."*

In the following viewpoint, author Rob Moll interviews President Mark Earley of the Prison Fellowship, a faith-based rehabilitation program that supports prisoners during and after their sentences. According to Earley, programs of this kind have been very successful in preparing prisoners to re-enter society with the spiritual support and practical training they need. Faith-based programs have also significantly lowered the numbers of re-arrests after sentences have been completed, says Earley. Even as legal burdens fall to the Prison Fellowship, ministries continue their programs in the United States and abroad. Author Rob Moll is an associate editor for Christianity Today.

GUIDED READING QUESTIONS:
1. How does Mark Earley interpret Jesus' words in Matthew 25 of the Bible?
2. In which states has the InnerChange Freedom Initiative established programs?

Rob Moll, "Rx for Recidivism: Prison Fellowship President Mark Earley Talks about Challenges the Ministry Faces," *Christianity Today*, vol. 50, November 2006, pp. 70-75. Copyright © 2006 by *Christianity Today*, Inc. Reproduced by permission of the author.

3. According to Earley, where does the future of prison ministry
   work lie?

This year, Prison Fellowship (PF) celebrates its 30th anniversary. Created in 1976 by Charles Colson after his release from prison for Watergate-related crimes [In 1972, a scandal involving government officials led to President Richard Nixon's resignation.], the organization now operates in 114 countries and is the largest prison ministry in the world. Last year, 24,531 PF volunteers supported by 16,797 churches ministered in 1,604 prisons in the United States. PF's related ministries, like Justice Fellowship, Angel Tree, and the Wilberforce Forum, work for safer prison conditions, religious freedom, the well-being of prisoners' families, and other issues, [Christianity Today] CT associate editor Rob Moll spoke with Prison Fellowship president Mark Earley about developments in prison ministry and legal challenges to its prisoner release program.

Times Have Changed
What is different about incarceration for the prisoner today versus the prisoner of 30 years ago?

One of the most significant changes in the criminal justice system over the last 30 years is the growth of the number of people in prison. When Chuck Colson founded Prison Fellowship in the mid-'70s, there were a quarter of a million people in prisons in the United States. Today that figure is 2.3 million. There's been a ten-fold increase over the last 30 years in the prison population.

Recidivism rates are staggering. Two-thirds of inmates will be re-arrested within three years of their release. With those numbers and with the public policy changes over the last 20 years that have incarcerated more people, we've had a ballooning prison population.

Disciples Behind Bars
How has Prison Fellowship addressed this rising prison population?

It has certainly been a growing mission field. Prison Fellowship's response, both in the United States and around the world, has been to seek to mobilize the church to believe what Jesus said in Matthew 25, that if you visit a prisoner, you visit him.

We help the church understand our responsibilities as congregations and as individuals to be involved in making disciples behind bars and [helping] those disciples [as they] come out of prison. We welcome them back into society, particularly those who have been changed by Christ and need a church home, a Bible study group, a mentor.

Success in Texas

One program you run to prepare prisoners for release is the InnerChange Freedom Initiative, which recently lost a court battle. What does that program do and what court challenges are you facing?

Prison Fellowship launched the InnerChange Freedom Initiative ten years ago in Texas to try to deal with the problem of recidivism. The concept was based loosely on a program in Brazil in which the authorities pretty much turned the keys of a prison over to the local Catholic parish and said, "We can't do anything with this place; see if you can."

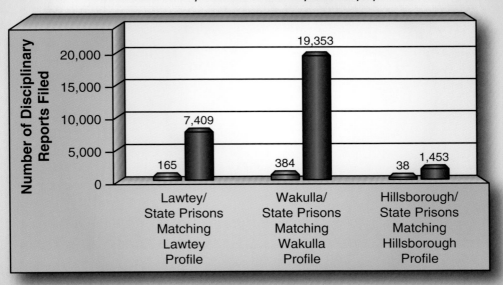

Faith-Based Prisons Work

Three Florida faith-based prisons (Lawtey, Wakulla, and Hillsborough) filed significantly fewer disciplinary reports than did state prisons with comparable populations.

Taken from: "Faith-and Character-Based Initiative, March 2007 Update," Florida Department of Corrections.

The prison became a model of transformation.

Twelve years ago, folks from the Texas Department of Corrections and leaders at Prison Fellowship visited the Brazilian program. We decided to try something similar in Texas.

The InnerChange Freedom Initiative is a pre-release program that works with inmates for two years prior to their release and one year after their release. Two hundred men live together in a faith-based, holistic program. It's not only based on spiritual transformation. It also includes academic training, vocational training, life skills training, substance abuse treatment, and post-prison assistance with employment and getting rooted into a local church. Every prisoner is assigned a mentor who will work with them both in prison and when they leave the prison. The program is now in six states—Texas, Iowa, Kansas, Minnesota, Arkansas, and Missouri.

The program in Texas was studied by the University of Pennsylvania, which confirmed a study by the Texas Department of Criminal Justice. The studies showed that those who graduated from the program had

Spritiual belief systems can be an integral part of criminal rehabilitation.

a 17 percent re-arrest rate and an 8 percent re-incarceration rate after two years. That's a pretty dramatic decrease in recidivism.

However, if people come into the program and drop out, their recidivism rates aren't any better than in the general prison population. Unless you finish it, you're not going to be able to read very well.

Legal Problems

We were sued in Iowa three years ago after operating for about seven years with no legal challenges. We were sued by Barry Lynn and Americans United for Separation of Church and State. The judge ruled in June, and it couldn't have been any more adverse. He ordered that the program be shutdown in 60 days. He ordered that the Prison Fellowship pay back all of the money that it had received from the state of Iowa, which amounts to $1.7 million.

He also took it upon himself to define evangelicals as distinct from other Christian groups. He said that the views that evangelicals hold on the substitutionary atonement and bodily resurrection of Christ are not widely held by Christians. And it led him to the conclusion that there's nothing that an evangelical can do or say that isn't aimed at converting someone. Based on that, he found the program was not constitutional.

We've appealed the case, and while that is pending, the judge's order to shut down the program and pay back the money we've received from the state is on hold.

Support of Churches

How have churches responded to your attempts to get them more involved in prison ministry?

When Chuck got ready to found Prison Fellowship, he says Billy Graham told him. "Why don't you preach, because you're going to have a hard time getting the church to embrace a ministry to prisoners."

Today, there are hundreds and hundreds of local churches that have their own prison ministries. There are great organizations like Good News Jail and Prison Ministry, Kairos Prison Ministry, and Bill Glass's Champions for Life. The combined effort of all of us working together is that we see churches today much more willing to embrace prison ministry than they were 30 years ago.

The church fundamentally views prisoners differently than the secular world, because they have been created in the image of God.

Needs of the Prisoners

How does that translate to Prison Fellowship's public policy work?

Justice Fellowship works on restorative justice, which is an attempt to bring biblical principles to bear on the criminal justice system at large: how the criminal justice system views inmates, how it views the justice process, how it understands the notion of justice, how it views restitution and punishment, how it views the needs of the victim.

Are you working on any particular piece of legislation?

We're working on legislation on Capitol Hill called the Second Chance Act. It's a bipartisan bill that creates grants for states and community groups to work with prisoners who are being released.

The future of prison ministry lies in working with those who are coming out of prison. For many years, a lot of people viewed prison ministry as what goes on when someone is in prison. What we're finding is that if we want to see God continue to raise up men and women from within prison, see them come to Christ, make lifestyle changes, and be fruitful for the rest of their lives after they get out of prison, some of the most critical ministry occurs when they leave the prison gate.

A lot of our energy is being devoted to that critical period. When a prisoner comes out of prison, he is as vulnerable if not more vulnerable than in prison.

Criminals off the Streets

If more people are in prison, that's fewer people on the streets committing crimes. Is an increase in prison population a bad thing?

There's an attitude that says we're going to solve social problems by putting more people in jail. Obviously that's not working, because the vast majority of these people are not entering society better off. What goes on in prison doesn't stay in prison. It spills out into the community.

A second thing that's contributed to that has been minimum mandatory sentences that take away the discretion of judges. That has proven not to be a good idea. We have instituted minimum mandatory sentences for a whole range of offenses, and it has resulted in long sentences and taken away judges' discretion to fashion the sentence based on the crime.

I understand there has been a dramatic increase in female prisoners.

A lot of it has to do with drugs, a lot of it has to do with methamphetamine abuse. It's tragic. Going into a men's unit is tragic enough. Going into a women's unit is doubly tragic, because almost all of them have children, and the shame that they bear for being separated from their children, is a heavy, heavy burden.

Overseas Ministries
What is Prison Fellowship's overseas ministry?

All of our overseas ministries are independently funded and independently chartered. So Prison Fellowship is not a missionary organization in the old-fashioned use of the word. People in those countries said, "We want to start a Prison Fellowship ministry in Ghana, in Bolivia, in Costa Rica." They begin the program and they fund it. Their staff is indigenous. and their funding is indigenous. It's a model that has allowed for rapid expansion. It hasn't been plagued by East-West, North-South cultural differences that American missionaries often run into.

Our ministry looks very different in every country. But we share a common statement of faith, and we share a common objective to reach out to prisoners.

EVALUATING THE AUTHOR'S ARGUMENTS:

Author Rob Moll presents the arguments for faith-based prisons as beneficial to society. How might he further support these programs against the counter-argument that they violate the separation of church and state?

Faith-Based Prisons Should Be Illegal

Rob Boston

"It's both unconstitutional and morally wrong for the government to pressure inmates to convert to evangelical Christianity as the price of obtaining rehabilitation services."

In the following viewpoint author Rob Boston reports on a lawsuit against the InnerChange Freedom Initiative (IFI), a faith-based prison rehabilitation program, filed on the grounds that the program is a violation of church and state. Inmates should not have to be pressured to convert to evangelical Christianity to have access to rehabilitation programs, argues Boston. Secondly, IFI's evangelical beliefs, such as the immorality of homosexuality and the denunciation of other religions, are not appropriate for a public setting such as a prison. Finally, IFI's success rates are falsified, according to Boston; inmates who went through the faith-based rehab program actually returned to prison in higher numbers than other inmates. For these reasons, faith-based rehabilitation programs should be illegal, the author concludes.

Rob Boston is the editor of *Church and State* magazine, the official publication of Americans United for Separation of Church and State.

Rob Boston, "Iowa Inmate Indoctrination on Trial," *Church and State,* December 1, 2005. Reproduced by permission.

AS YOU READ, CONSIDER THE FOLLOWING QUESTIONS:
1. Why do attorneys for the Americans United for Separation of Church and State call IFI "a government-funded conversion program?"
2. What is the tone of money management and job seeking classes offered by IFI, according to the author?
3. Why are claims that IFI reduces prisoner recidivism statistically invalid, as reported by Boston?

A select group of inmates at central Iowa's Newton Correctional Facility has been learning some controversial things lately.

They're being told that the Bible ordains men to run households; that homosexuality is a sin; that non-Christian religions are "of Satan" and that only persons baptized as adults can get into Heaven.

Thanks to the Iowa legislature and officials at the Iowa Department of Corrections, the inmates are learning all of this courtesy of the taxpayers. But the taxpayers may be relieved of this burden soon, thanks to a lawsuit filed by Americans United for Separation of Church and State.

Taxpayer-Funded Religion

Newton, a medium-security institution with about 900 inmates, has been sponsoring a controversial evangelical Christian indoctrination program called the InnerChange Freedom Initiative since 1999. Founded by ex-Watergate felon Charles W. Colson's Prison Fellowship Ministries, InnerChange seeks to rehabilitate prisoners by convening them to one ultra-conservative form of Christianity. . . .

Americans United attorneys examined InnerChange and became convinced that it was a clear example of taxpayer-funded religion. When Iowa corrections officials refused to drop its sponsorship, Americans United filed suit to block further public subsidies. . . .

"InnerChange is essentially a government-funded conversion program," said Americans United Executive Director Barry W. Lynn. "Prison Fellowship is free to run evangelism programs on its own dime but has no business handing the bill to the taxpayers. This set-up clearly violates the separation of church and state."

Faith-based rehabilitation programs in prisons may violate the inmate's religious beliefs.

During opening arguments Oct. 24, [2005] Americans United Senior Litigation Counsel Alex Luchenitser told the court that the religious nature of InnerChange is undeniable.

"InnerChange has taken over an entire unit of a state prison and turned it into an evangelical church," Luchenitser said. . . .

Discriminating Against Inmates of All Faiths

Muslim inmate Bobby Shelton said he also concluded that the program is hostile to his spirtual perspective. "There is no possible way for me as a Sunni Muslim to participate without blaspheming my faith, blaspheming God," Shelton testified.

Prison and InnerChange officials contend that InnerChange is open to all inmates.

Technically that's true. But there's a catch: The program is so saturated in Colson's version of evangelical Christianity that members of other faiths are unlikely to feel comfortable taking part. For inmates, the choice is either to grin and bear it and subject themselves to constant proselytization or skip the program.

Evangelical teachings pervade the material used by InnerChange staff. One class, called "Heart of the Problem," is designed to help inmates understand "there is no human remedy for sin and the only cure is Christ. . . ." The course's goal is to introduce "members to the concept of healthy spiritual living."

Another class, "Old and New Testament Literature," lists its goal as to "introduce the member to the person of Jesus Christ as the Son of God and Savior" and "to understand their new identity as a member of the body of Christ."

Even classes that deal with secular topics such as money management and job seeking are anchored to evangelical principles. A class called "Financial Management," which is designed to help inmates manage money, states that it will "bluntly inform the inmate of the primary biblical principal [sic] as stated in the book of Psalms, 'the earth is the LORD'S and everything in it.' This includes his money."

"Catholics Aren't Really Christians"

The promotion of evangelical Christianity often comes at the expense of other faiths. At trial and during discovery, Luchenitser and other attorneys for AU took testimony from inmates who reported that InnerChange personnel made derogatory comments about Catholicism, Judaism, Islam and other religions.

One inmate reported during discovery that an InnerChange staffer told him, "Catholics aren't really Christians." Another inmate wrote in his journal, "Today we had some serious Catholic bashing in class. It hurt me very deeply. Never before had I heard serious criticism toward my faith. Spent the rest of the day trying to sort it out in my . . . mind and put away the bitterness."

At trial, inmates testified that InnerChange personnel likened the pope to Hitler and to the Antichrist. Other inmates testified that InnerChange staff asked Catholics not to read from their version of the Bible. A manual used in the program advised readers to be wary of "pronouncements of church officials such as bishops, cardinals, popes."

According to one inmate, Catholic inmates who protested against such practices "either left on their own or were asked to leave."

Another InnerChange book goes beyond Catholic bashing and includes a "Spiritual checklist" of groups to be wary of. Islam, Hinduism, Mormonism, Unitarianism, Jehovah's Witnesses, Christian Science, New Age, Buddhism, Bahaism and Native American faiths all made the roster.

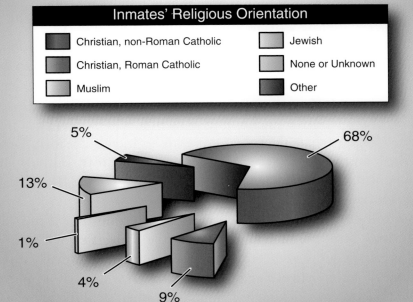

Inmates Have Many Faiths

Data taken at the Faith-and Character-Based Institutions of Lawtey, Wakulla and Hillsborough CI, in Florida, found that inmate religious affiliations are diverse. Some claim that faith-based programs are inappropriate and even unconstitutional in such religiously diverse environments.

Inmates' Religious Orientation

- Christian, non-Roman Catholic
- Christian, Roman Catholic
- Muslim
- Jewish
- None or Unknown
- Other

5%
68%
13%
1%
4%
9%

Taken from: "Faith- and Character-Based Initiative, March 2007 Update," Florida Department of Corrections.

An Evangelical Agenda in a Public Institution

Further evidence of InnerChange's sectarian nature is found in its teachings on family life. During discovery, AU attorneys found workbooks used by InnerChange staff that instruct inmates that men have a biblical duty to run their households.

"Wives, submit to your own husbands, as to the Lord," reads one manual. "For the husband is head of the wife, as also Christ is head of the church. . . ." The manual goes on to call husbands the spiritual decision-makers or "heads" of the family and advises, "Wives are to submit to their husbands in this, just as the church submits to God."

Gay inmates were told that their behavior is sinful and advised that sexual orientation can be changed through religious conversion. Books used in the program condemn homosexuality as an "abomination" and a tool used by Satan to mislead. . . .

Falsified Rehabilitation Rates

How did a program with such sectarian goals find its way into a state prison? A slick sales pitch from Prison Fellowship may account for part of the answer. Corrections officials are always looking for programs to reduce recidivism among inmates. Colson's InnerChange has made startling claims of success, asserting that huge numbers of participants became law-abiding citizens after leaving prison.

In 2003, Colson released what he said was statistical validation for this claim. Prison Fellowship trumpeted a study that claimed to show that inmates who took part in InnerChange returned to prison at a much lower rate than those who did not.

The media reported the findings as factual, and Colson went to the White House to share the good news with his friends President George W. Bush and then Attorney General John Ashcroft. Bush, a faith-based enthusiast, asked Ashcroft to look for ways the InnerChange program could be expanded in federal prisons.

But it didn't take long for Colson's inflated claims to collapse. Mark Kleiman, a professor of public policy at the University of California-Los Angeles, examined the study and found it to be statistically invalid. Prison Fellowship had excluded all the prisoners who did not finish the program, in essence kicking its failures out. When all of the participants were added back in, Kleiman found that InnerChange participants actually returned to prison at a slightly higher rate than a control group.

Rehabilitation Should Not Be Tied to Religion

None of this has slowed down InnerChange's growth. The program receives tax support in Texas, Kansas and Minnesota, and another program is in the works in Arkansas. (Florida runs two "faith-based" prisons that are not officially connected with InnerChange.)

Americans United's Lynn stresses that AU does not oppose rehabilitative programs for prisoners. In fact, Lynn said he believes state support for InnerChange runs counter to the goal of rehabilitation by offering a program so steeped in one religious perspective that many inmates do not feel comfortable taking part.

An inmate's opportunity for rehabilitation, AU lawyers say, should not hinge on his or her willingness to adopt evangelical Christianity. . . .

"It's both unconstitutional and morally wrong for the government to pressure inmates to convert to evangelical Christianity as the price of obtaining rehabilitation services," Lynn observed. "It is in the public interest for inmates to receive the best rehabilitation possible, so that they can make a contribution to society when they leave prison. But no American should be strong-armed by the government to adopt a particular religious viewpoint."

EVALUATING THE AUTHORS' ARGUMENTS:

Author Rob Boston and Byron R. Johnson disagree that faith-based programs should be used to rehabilitate prisoners. After reading both viewpoints, with which author do you agree? Explain your reasoning and support your answer with evidence from the text.

Chapter 2

How Should Inmates Be Treated?

Health care and prison labor are some of the topics discussed in prison reform debates.

Prisons Should Use Inmate Labor

Rob Atkinson and Knut A. Rostad

"There are a number of benefits from inmate work programs, including enhanced institutional security, reduced recidivism for inmates, an available workforce for business, lower public service costs for taxpayers, and finally, increased economic output for society."

In the following viewpoint authors Rob Atkinson and Knut A. Rostad argue on behalf of prison labor programs. The authors claim that such programs reduce unrest and violence in prisons by busying inmates with something to focus on. Furthermore, work programs give inmates valuable job training, which helps them become employed once they are released from prison. Their ability to find employment reduces offender recidivism, or the tendency of criminals to re-offend and be sent to jail again in the future. Atkinson and Rostad further report that employers who use prison labor find it to be a high quality and motivated workforce, and more productive than a regular workforce. Finally, the authors argue that prison work programs are a fair way to make inmates pay for the cost of incarcerating them, thousands of dollars which otherwise is paid by taxpayers. For these reasons Atkinson and Rostad conclude that prisoners, employers, and the general public benefit from prison work programs.

Rob Atkinson and Knut A. Rostad, "Can Inmates Become an Integral Part of the U.S. Workforce?" Urban Institute Reentry Roundtable, May 19-20, 2003. Reproduced by permission.

Rob Atkinson is an analyst with the Progressive Policy Institute. Knut A. Rostad is an analyst with the Enterprise Prison Institute.

AS YOU READ, CONSIDER THE FOLLOWING QUESTIONS:
1. What U.S. politician has petitioned for inmate labor programs on the grounds that it helps reduce unrest in prisons, according to the authors?
2. What percentage of participants in a 1991 study of ex-inmates who participated in prison work programs found and kept jobs, as reported by the author?
3. What percentage of employers said they would recommend the use of prison labor to business associates, according to the authors?

American jails and prisons, for the first time in history, now hold more than 2,000,000 inmates. . . . The most recent data shows that more than two thirds of all state ex-offenders are re-arrested in three years. One successful program that has demonstrated success in reducing recidivism is prison work in industries. Yet, only 7% of state and federal inmates work in industries programs—despite compelling evidence that such programs benefit inmates, public safety and the economy as a whole. . . . Reforming the current Federal Prison Industries program by opening up prisons to greater private sector prison employment is good public policy that can over come resistance. . . .

There are a number of benefits from inmate work programs, including enhanced institutional security, reduced recidivism for inmates, an available workforce for business, lower public service costs for taxpayers, and finally, increased economic output for society.

Work Programs Reduce Unrest in Prisons

The significance of inmate work in maintaining institutional security is unquestioned among prison administrators. Routinely, administrators use the term "management tool" and industries almost interchangeably. Prison disturbances are commonly explained as a result of a lack of work programs. Former Federal Bureau of Prisons (FBOP)

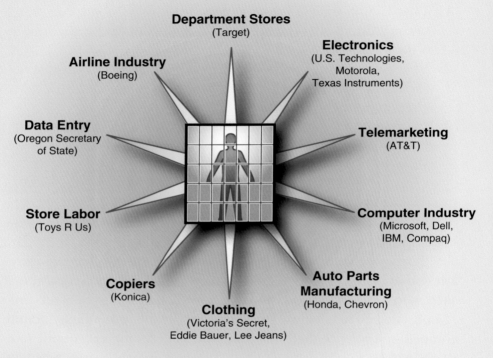

Uses for Prison Labor

A variety of companies use or have recently used prison labor to make a multitude of products.

Department Stores
(Target)

Electronics
(U.S. Technologies, Motorola, Texas Instruments)

Airline Industry
(Boeing)

Data Entry
(Oregon Secretary of State)

Telemarketing
(AT&T)

Store Labor
(Toys R Us)

Computer Industry
(Microsoft, Dell, IBM, Compaq)

Copiers
(Konica)

Auto Parts Manufacturing
(Honda, Chevron)

Clothing
(Victoria's Secret, Eddie Bauer, Lee Jeans)

Source: Compiled by editor from multiple sources.

director James Bennett attributed disturbances in federal prisons in the early 1930s to a lack of work, as were state prison riots in the early 1950s also said to show the "absolute necessity for a well-planned and comprehensive work and production program." In 1979, former Senator Charles Percy explained the need for the federal legislation to authorize the Prison Industry Enhancement program by recounting the "night-marish reality" of a prison riot in Potomac, Illinois. More recently, the importance of industries to institutional security is a constant theme in testimony of FBOP officials before Congress, and members of Congress seeking to reform the program fully acknowledge this issue.

As an unquestioned "law" of prison administration, the correlation between inmate work programs and institutional security has not received significant attention from researchers. The FBOP Post Release Employment Project (PREP) study may be the best known study of impact of industries experiences on exoffenders' employment. It concluded that industries inmates were less likely to have a misconduct report, less likely to have a serious misconduct report and more likely to be rated as possessing a higher level of responsibility.

A Chance for Inmates to Better Themselves

There is broad agreement that employment in industries provide important benefits to inmates. Three types of benefits are mentioned most often. First, reducing idleness helps inmates (as well as administrators and staff) by reducing tension within the institution. Second, depending on the nature of the work, work allows inmates to learn workplace habits, practices and readiness skills. In better jobs, inmates also learn specific and relevant job and vocational skills. . . . Moreover, the wages inmates earn helps inmates and their dependents financially, emotionally and psychologically.

Finally, studies on inmate tracking indicate that rates of recidivism or re-arrests are lower for inmates with industries work experience than for inmates without this experience. In 1991 the FBOP released an analysis of PREP. More than 7,000 program participants were evaluated over a two-year period. The study found that those offenders who received training and work experience while in prison had fewer conduct problems and were less likely to be arrested the first year after release. The study also found that upon release prison workers were 24% more likely to obtain a full-time or day-labor job during this time. Moreover, by the end of the first year of release year, 10.1% of the comparison group inmates had been re-arrested or had their conditional release revoked, compared with 6.6% of the program participants. Further, 72% of the program participants found and maintained employment during this period, compared with just 63% of the comparison group inmates. The study concludes that "It appears that prison employment in an industrial work setting and vocational or apprenticeship training can have both short- and long-term effects that reduce the likelihood of recidivism, particularly for men. . . Therefore, correctional

Helping the community and learning new skills is often the goal of inmate labor programs.

industries work and training programs could help to reduce prison populations.". . .

A Quality and Motivated Workforce

For many years, the benefits to businesses from employing inmates has been in question. . . . [But] in 2002, the Enterprise Prison Institute completed a field survey of inmate employers to explore some of these issues. The survey of inmate employers sought to attain an understanding of their views of the strengths and weaknesses of employing this workforce as compared to an alternative domestic workforce.

Two conclusions stand out from the data. First, employers regard inmate workers as a quality workforce; secondly, they believe inmates receive valuable training.

After having employed inmates for an average of about six years, employers believe that the inmate workforce is a quality workforce. . . .

Additionally, employers rated inmates as somewhat more productive than a domestic workforce might be, and 92% said they "recommend" the inmate workforce to business associates. As one employer explains: "Inmates learn that the success of our company depends on the satisfaction of our customers with our product. Quality, service and price have to meet expectations. Our futures are intertwined. They are justly proud of what we have accomplished.". . .

Everyone Benefits

Employers provide inmates training that is significant and valuable.

While measuring the individual or economic value of the skills training was beyond the scope of the field survey, the survey queried employers' views on training. These findings provide support for concluding that inmates learn important skills in these jobs, and corroborate anecdotal evidence that prisons can provide an effective job-training environment. In describing what inmates learn, there is significant emphasis on workplace skills; i.e.: issues of "teamwork, dependability, pride, job readiness, communications" accounting for 64% of the responses.

The value of this training appears significant. The skills inmates attain while employed in prison appear to parallel what the National Association of Manufacturers (NAM) members claim their production workers lack—"basic employability skills.". . .

Paying their Way

Taxpayers can also benefit from inmate work if a portion of the revenue from prison work goes to pay for the costs of housing prisoners and to pay for victim restitution, child support and the like. Indeed, the majority of Americans support inmate labor because they believe that prisoners should help offset some of the costs of incarceration. It costs approximately $40 billion annually to incarcerate prisoners in local, state and federal prisons. That works out to approximately $20,000 a year per prisoner. Surely prisoners can work and contribute something to help pay for this so that taxpayers don't have to pay as much. Opponents of inmate labor use the fact that some inmate laborers are lifers with no chance of release to argue that the focus on reduced recidivism is just a sham. The fact is that requiring a lifer to work and contribute a portion of his pay to room and board is consistent with the notion of the prisoner's responsibility to give something back to society to pay for his crimes and costs to society of incarceration. . . .

There is a lot that can and should be done to make sure that workers and businesses benefit in the New Economy. Opposing inmate labor is not one of them. In fact, limiting inmate labor would lower economic growth, while reducing the effectiveness of prisons to move prisoners to productive and law-abiding lives when they are released.

EVALUATING THE AUTHOR'S ARGUMENTS:

Rob Atkinson and Knut A. Rostad claim that prison labor programs help inmates find employment once they are released. Would Kathy Kelly, author of the following viewpoint, agree with this claim? Why or why not?

Prisons Should Not Use Inmate Labor

Kathy Kelly

"We continue to lose good paying jobs to a government sponsored prison labor program."

Prison labor programs are unfair and wrong, writes author Kathy Kelly in the following viewpoint. According to Kelly, prison laborers are paid slave wages and do not learn skills that will help them get employed after they are released from prison. Furthermore, corporations exploit prison laborers by profiting enormously from their labor and not giving compensation, such as insurance, retirement benefits, or vacation, in return. Finally, prison labor takes jobs away from hard-working Americans who need to be paid fair wages, Kelly argues. For all of these reasons she denounces prison labor as immoral and inappropriate.

Kathy Kelly is an American peace activist. She is currently co-coordinator of the nonprofit organization Voices for Creative Nonviolence.

AS YOU READ, CONSIDER THE FOLLOWING QUESTIONS:

1. How many prison laborers are employed in the United States, and how much are they typically paid, as reported by Kelly?

Kathy Kelly, "US Prison Labor: Another Cog in the War Machine," antiwar.com, May 7, 2004. Reproduced by permission of the author.

2. Why are prison laborers not likely to find employment once they are released from jail, according to the author?
3. What job-draining phenomenon did Senator Craig Thomas compare prison labor programs to, according to Kelly?

I t's Saturday morning, May 1, 2004, and women here at Pekin Federal Prison Camp who watched CNN news feel indignant about the way Iraqi prisoners have been treated by US military guards. "Did you see those pictures?" Ruth asked. What in the world is going on over there?"

The news coverage they watched had photo-ops from last year's May Day, when President George Bush triumphantly boarded a

Entrusting inmates with the upkeep of historical cemetery markers may not be in the public's best interest.

FAST FACT

Prisoners are usually paid minimum wage for jobs they perform. But 80 percent of their salary must be donated to victims' rights organizations, state restitution funds, anti-drug campaigns, and to an inmate trust fund, leaving about 20 percent for the prisoner. The Prison Activist Resource Center estimates that most prisoners make under $.20 per hour, and some don't get paid at all.

USS Carrier ship to declare "Mission Accomplished," juxtaposed with the recently released ghastly photos of US military members apparently enjoying degradation and torture of Iraqi prisoners.

"Where did May Day traditions come from?" I later asked aloud, in the prison library. The librarian, Lori, quickly found an Encyclopedia item detailing various May Day traditions. Several of us laughed about one which holds that the dew on the grass, on May 1, holds special qualities for restoring youth. Authorities would be mighty surprised if we all started rolling on the grass. "It would be better to celebrate morning dew than to boast about dropping all those bombs over Iraq," said Carol. "Looks like people there are going to hate us so much, they'd rather kill us than look at us."

Prisoners Work for Slave Wages

Discussion turned to an April 7, 2004 press release which arrived in yesterday's mail. Issued by the American Federal Government Employees union, it urges members to lobby against Senate Bill 346, introduced by Senators Carl Levin and Craig Thomas. The bill proposes rescinding federal contracting preferences for Federal Prison Industries (FPI).

The FPI, or UNICOR, was begun in 1934, under President Franklin Roosevelt, as a program to keep prisoners busy and equip them with job skills in preparation for release. It now employs 21,000 prisoners. The UNICOR workers earn hourly rates ranging from 0.23 to $1.23. Much of that money goes back into prison related industry if the prison laborers buy highly priced commissary items or make regular phone calls which cost 0.25 per minute.

At the Federal Correctional Institute (FCI) medium high security men's prison adjacent to this camp, and at many other FCIs, the UNICOR factories operate 24 hours per day, employing three shifts of prison laborers.

Taking Advantage of Inmates

The laborers may be learning new skills, but their experience won't guarantee them jobs on "the outside" where they are not allowed to even list UNICOR as a reference. Imagine telling a prospective employer that you have 15 years of experience as a welder, but can't supply a reference. And you're an ex-con.

I don't think the American Federal Government Employees union cares, primarily, about helping prisoners "while away the hours" or prepare for employment after being released. A clue about their interests in maintaining UNICOR lies in the fact that the only ones who can hold a share in UNICOR profits are federal employees. Since the FPI/ UNICOR doesn't have to compete with any other industry to procure federal contracts, they can charge any price they want for the products or services they supply. One prisoner here is helping make chains for light switches at her UNICOR job. Each chain is sold for $32.00.

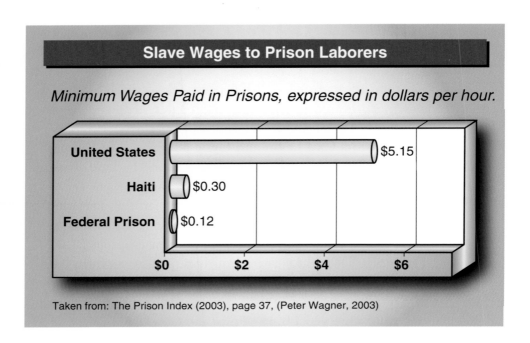

Slave Wages to Prison Laborers

Minimum Wages Paid in Prisons, expressed in dollars per hour.

United States	$5.15
Haiti	$0.30
Federal Prison	$0.12

$0 $2 $4 $6

Taken from: The Prison Index (2003), page 37, (Peter Wagner, 2003)

UNICOR factories use antiquated equipment, have a hard time meeting deadlines, and aren't subject to much quality control. If they were forced to be competitive with outside industries, many within the prison system forecast that UNICOR wouldn't last long. However, under the present conditions, UNICOR is a profitable company. The wages are low, the client base (the US federal government) is guaranteed, and there's no need to worry about paying company insurance, retirement benefits, or vacation pay. Nor is the FPI/UNICOR subject to compliance with OSHA regulations.

Prison Labor Takes Jobs from American

"Prisoners are responsible for producing a diverse range of products," stated Senator Craig Thomas before the Senate Committee on Governmental affairs, on April 7, 2004, "ranging from office furniture to clothing, from electronics to eyewear, from military gear to call centers and laundry services, to mapping and engineering drafting."

"It is ironic," Senator Thomas continued, "that in recent months as we have been debating the issue of off-shoring of American jobs, we continue to lose good paying American jobs to a government sponsored prison labor program."

In a Harper's Magazine article, Ian Urbina reports that "FPI, the federal government's 39th largest contractor, sells more than $400 million worth of products to the US military." (October 2003) Prison laundries clean, press and repair uniforms. Prisoners manufacture helmets, shorts, underwear, flak jackets and ammunition.

Prison Labor Is Unfair and Wrong

On May Day, 2003, when President Bush proudly outfitted himself in military clothing, posing for a photo-op to proclaim "Mission Accomplished," did he wear clothing manufactured by forced laborers in US prisons?

This May, remembering the "Mission Accomplished" banner displayed behind President Bush a year ago, we need to ask ourselves very carefully, while listening to the stories of prisoners here and abroad, what is the mission? What has been accomplished?

EVALUATING THE AUTHORS' ARGUMENTS:

Authors Kathy Kelly and Rob Atkinson and Knut Rostad disagree on whether prison labor programs are good or bad. After reading both viewpoints, what do you think? Should prisons use inmate labor programs? In your opinion, who largely benefits from them? Explain your answer using examples from the texts you have read.

Viewpoint 3

Prisoner Health Care Is Inadequate

James Sterngold

"Inmates shouldn't die before they have a chance for parole. They shouldn't be given a life sentence because they can't get health care."

In the following viewpoint, author James Sterngold reports on how overcrowding and under funding in American prisons results in inadequate health care for inmates. He describes conditions at California's Soledad prison, which, with a shortage of beds, doctors, nurses, and medical equipment, fails to provide acceptable health care to the more than 7,000 inmates housed at the facility. Sterngold reports that because inmates are wards of the state, they are supposed to be guaranteed health care, yet many suffer from treatable illnesses and even die from preventable diseases. James Sterngold is a staff writer for the San Francisco Chronicle, from which this viewpoint was taken.

AS YOU READ, CONSIDER THE FOLLOWING QUESTIONS:

1) According to the author, how many inmates was Soledad state prison built for? How many does it currently hold?
2) Name three diseases commonly found in prisons, as reported by Sterngold.
3) What does overcrowding contribute to prison infirmary problems, as described in the viewpoint?

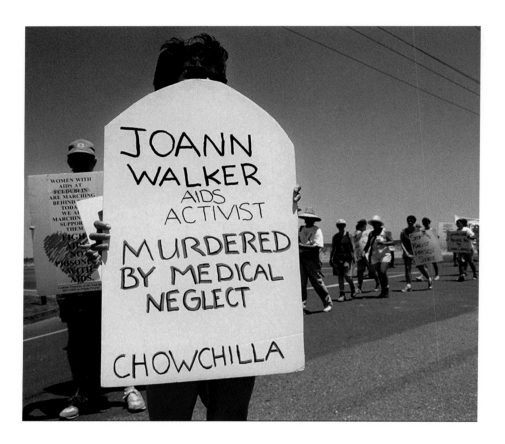

Activists protesting substandard health care and support services for female prisoners point out that female prisoners have died from medical neglect.

As the medical staff at the Correctional Training Facility prison gathered recently for its morning meeting, doctors and nurses let loose with another day's frustrations.

A team of guards had shown up unannounced and cleared the infirmary of all black inmates that morning, to avoid fistfights with several Latinos coming in for X-rays. Racial violence has been growing in the badly crowded prison, which was built for 2,815 inmates but holds 7,000. The incursion worsened an already severe appointment backlog.

Then there was the local hospital that wanted to send back an inmate dying of liver disease. The prison didn't have facilities to care for him—the reason he'd been sent to the hospital twice before, at a cost to taxpayers of $50,877.75 for just 11 days. The staff was scrambling to find a prison that could take him.

Last, the head nurse explained that the infirmary had signed a contract for a mobile CAT scan to come to the prison, instead of transporting inmates to hospitals at high cost. But four months later, it had yet to make a visit because of a dispute over how it would be guarded. (Resolving the problem took several more weeks.)

"They are making one costly error after another, and the problems just get more monstrous," said Dr. Michael Friedman, the chief medical officer. "They keep taking away our tools and telling us to do more."

The infirmary at Soledad, the state's largest prison, provides far from the worst level of medical care. But a day there offered insight into why a federal judge ruled this year that the health care in California's prison system is so bad it violates inmates' constitutional protection against cruel and unusual punishment.

Repairing years of mismanagement by the Corrections Department could cost hundreds of millions of dollars, over the $1.1 billion a year taxpayers already spend on prison health care.

Because of substance abuse problems, violence and often impoverished backgrounds, prison inmates are among the sickest people in the state.

The staff at Soledad treats inmates who have high levels of chronic diseases such as diabetes, asthma and hypertension and near-epidemic levels of infectious diseases like hepatitis C, and who suffer violent injuries as prison crowding stokes tensions.

As courts hand down longer sentences under "three strikes" and other tough laws, medical staffs also see a growing number of geriatric inmates, many of whom require expensive treatments, even organ transplants.

But the staff also faces the constraints of prison conditions and the bureaucratic failures of the Corrections Department. In prison after prison, the result is critical shortages of doctors and nurses, plummeting morale and growing numbers of preventable deaths.

When inmates aren't properly treated, they return to their communities with costly ailments or carrying communicable diseases.

Unlike most Americans, however, inmates are guaranteed adequate health care. California's prison system has not only failed to provide that minimal level of care, it also has failed repeatedly, in spite of many court mandates and numerous promises of improvements.

Now a federal district judge, Thelton Henderson, is taking control of what is one of the largest health care systems in the country, providing medical treatment for the state's 165,000 inmates.

He is expected to appoint a receiver soon to make changes that experts say could end up costing taxpayers billions over the next decade to do everything from repairing filthy and inadequate facilities to computerizing medical records to paying bonuses to attract qualified professionals.

"By all accounts, the California prison medical care system is broken beyond repair," Henderson wrote in issuing his order this month.

"The harm already done in this case to California's prison inmate population could not be more grave, and the threat of future injury and death is virtually guaranteed in the absence of drastic action." ...

At Soledad, the infirmary looks much like any small clinic, neat and well lighted. There is a single guard at the heavy metal entry door.

The waiting room is a series of benches inside a heavy chain-link fence. And the inmates, who show up for appointments right after breakfast, come prepared to wait, most bringing lunches stuffed into clear plastic bags.

Inmates can enter the infirmary only with a special permission slip, called a ducat, and they say the politics of getting those precious slips is a time-consuming game.

The wait hints at the underlying issue: overcrowding. The prison holds 21/2 times as many inmates as it was designed for, and it shows.

A few yards down a corridor from the infirmary is what was once a gym. Now 120 bunk beds are bolted to the floor. All the day rooms along the corridor have been filled with bunks, too.

The infirmary, meanwhile, has been shrinking. Jim Anderson, 63, a longtime nurse who is officially retired but was brought back as a consultant, said that when he started work at Soledad in 1980, the infirmary had 32 beds for a population of less than 3,000; now, for 7,000 inmates, there are 16 beds. ...

The inmates said that because it can take so long to get medical appointments, and because the queues at the infirmary are so long, many inmates refused to go. That meant greater costs later as some illnesses—everything from asthma or infections to hypertension—went untreated.

"I can tell you, there's so little space and such a strain on the system, people don't want to come in," said John Thibeault, a council member who is serving 25 years to life for narcotics possession under California's "three strikes" law.

He nodded toward the jammed waiting room.

"That cage is like a dog kennel," he said. "The guy next to you could have something infectious. Some disabled guy has to climb over everyone to get out. Nobody wants to go through that."

Friedman, who joined the facility in 1999 and previously spent 15 years as a military doctor, responded firmly that the crowding was a fact of life.

In short, he said, he was seeking more space, but there was nothing to be done in the short term, and he warned that inmates using stratagems to see doctors early would just make the waits longer for other inmates.

"It's not up to the inmate population to come up with solutions," said Rafael Maldonado, another council member. "You're always going to have frivolous complaints, frivolous litigation and so on. That's not the problem. The problem is severe overcrowding and understaffing."

He added, "We have the largest lifer population of any prison. The inmates shouldn't die before they have a chance for parole. They shouldn't be given a life sentence because they can't get health care."

EVALUATING THE AUTHOR'S ARGUMENTS:

James Sterngold's article reflects the belief that everyone, even criminals, deserves basic medical care. In your opinion, should prisoners be entitled to adequate health care? Why or why not? Explain your reasoning.

Prisoner Health Care Is Too Generous

Michael Crowley

"Premium health care shouldn't be the reward for robbing a bank."

It is unfair that prisoners receive better health care than many Americans, argues author Michael Crowley in the following viewpoint. Crowley believes it is outrageous that taxpayers are forced to pay for inmates to receive organ transplants, plastic surgery, dialysis, and other top-shelf medical procedures. Average, upstanding Americans cannot afford such procedures, points out Crowley, and are even passed over for health care at the expense of inmates. Crowley concludes that prisoners should not be the recipients of the best health care America has to offer, especially at the expense of hard-working, law-abiding citizens. Michael Crowley, a regular columnist for *Reader's Digest*, is also an associate editor at *The New Republic* magazine.

GUIDED READING QUESTIONS:
1) Who is James Wolfe, as described by the author?
2) According to Crowley, how much did the state of Oregon spend on dialysis for a convicted murderer on death row?
3) What transplant did a twice-convicted felon in California receive, as reported by the author?

Michael Crowley, "Crime Pays…If you need top-notch medical care," *Reader's Digest*, October 2004. Reproduced by permission.

James Wolfe was doing hard time in Pennsylvania for raping an eight-year-old girl when he discovered that prison can be a pretty good deal. It seems James had always wanted to be a woman (he had even changed his name to Jessica), and a doctor labeled his condition "gender identity disorder." That made James eligible for hormone treatments to help change his gender—at taxpayer expense. The state says these treatments don't cost much, but according to an estimate by the Pittsburgh Tribune-Review, they can run up to $8,000 per year.

Here's the really bitter medicine: That amount could go a long way toward providing health insurance for a family. With an estimated 44 million people in America lacking health coverage, one million of them in Pennsylvania alone, you'd think inmates would be the

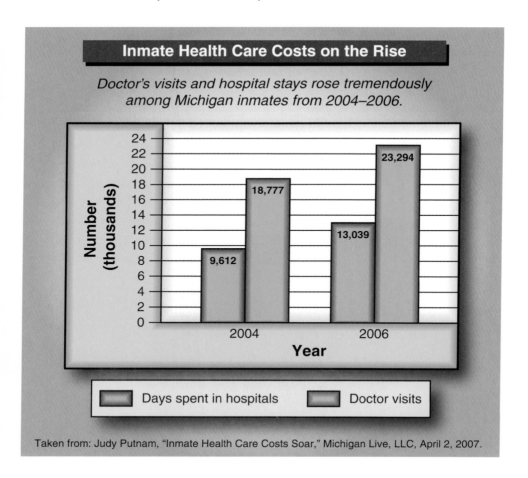

Inmate Health Care Costs on the Rise

Doctor's visits and hospital stays rose tremendously among Michigan inmates from 2004–2006.

Days spent in hospitals Doctor visits

Taken from: Judy Putnam, "Inmate Health Care Costs Soar," Michigan Live, LLC, April 2, 2007.

last to receive elective procedures. But Wolfe isn't the only criminal trying to get this sort of free treatment behind bars. Last year in New York State, for instance, a judge allowed a convicted murderer's lawsuit, demanding treatment for his gender identity disorder, to go forward. And in California this summer, an inmate allegedly got

a state-funded breast reduction operation. He happens to be a man. Plastic surgeons typically charge close to $3,000 for this procedure.

It gets worse because the problem goes well beyond these sorts of unusual treatments. Around the country, hardened criminals of every stripe receive top-notch care that many average families don't get, including expensive dental surgery. In Oregon, which has recently cut public health benefits, the state is spending about $120,000 per year on dialysis treatments for a convicted murderer on death row. In other words, it's shelling out big bucks to keep him alive until it's time to kill him. True, there's always the chance he'll get his death sentence revoked, but why are his costly treatments guaranteed and fully covered when plenty of law-abiding people can't afford the care they need?

Something to think about. So is the fact that other hugely expensive treatments, like bone marrow transplants and heart-bypass surgery, have been provided to prisoners, courtesy of your wallet and mine.

Convicts sometimes even qualify for precious organ transplants. Two years ago in California, a twice-convicted felon serving time for armed robbery got a new ticker, at an initial cost to the state of $900,000. At the time, 3,900 people were on the national waiting list for a new heart, and hundreds of them eventually died waiting. Meanwhile, a person without health insurance might never have made the list in the first place. Unlike an inmate with guaranteed coverage from the government, an uninsured individual may be judged too financially risky by many hospitals.

It's all startling evidence of a little-known quirk of American life: The only class of people with a constitutional right to health care in

Native Americans from reservations are quick to point out that their health care system is substandard to prison health care.

the United States are prison inmates. For the roughly one in seven Americans living without coverage, their best hope of seeing a doctor for free might be getting thrown behind bars. "Inmates are in the custody of the state, and it's our obligation to provide medical care to them," says Nick Lyman, a spokesman for the New York State corrections department.

How did it come to this? In 1976 the Supreme Court ruled that denying health care to inmates could amount to the "cruel and unusual" punishment prohibited by the U.S. Constitution. But thanks in part to a slew of prisoner lawsuits that have intimidated state officials, criminals often get care that others don't, or care that is far more than standard.

Take that California inmate who had breast surgery earlier this year. The prison's medical office insists that the inmate had a potentially cancerous lump removed. But state legislators had received a tip from a prison employee that the man was treated for overdevelopment of the breasts, possibly from steroid use, and legislators couldn't determine whether a biopsy was performed first. That was hardly the first case of its kind. "We found seven [breast reduction] cases in the last couple of years," says state assemblywoman Rebecca Cohn. Four of the seven procedures were done shortly before the inmates were released.

At times, the inmates even get top-dollar treatment. Cohn says the California state prison system spent $11 million for dermatology services in just one budget year—including services performed by a Beverly Hills dermatologist. The state has also spent millions on hearing aids for prisoners, even though many private health plans don't cover hearing aids. It's no wonder, then, that California's prison health care costs soared by 11 percent over the past year, even as its Medi-Cal program for the poor was chopped by almost $240 million.

Sure, this can be a tricky issue. Should we just let inmates die of illness without treatment? Does anyone want to deny a jailed shoplifter an emergency room visit? Of course not. But maybe it's time to ration care behind bars more carefully.

Maybe a violent criminal who needs a liver should be bumped down the long waiting list. And surely criminals shouldn't be rewarded with better coverage than law-abiding people, who deal with ever-stricter managed-care plans. The bottom line, though, is simply this: Premium health care shouldn't be the reward for robbing a bank.

EVALUATING THE AUTHOR'S ARGUMENTS:

Michael Crowley believes that inmates do not deserve to have access to premium health care, especially considering that law-abiding citizens often do not receive such high quality care. What do you think: Should the state draw the line at what kinds of procedures inmates are allowed to undergo? If you were in charge, what kinds of procedures would you allow and which would you rule as inappropriate?

Chapter 3

What Role Should Prisons Play in the War on Terror?

Soldiers stand side by side in uniform during the grand opening of a newly-refurbished prison in Afghanistan.

The Military Prison at Guantanamo Bay Should Be Closed

Bill Press

> *"Guantanamo Bay is a big black eye on the face of the United States, contradicting everything we supposedly stand for—in terms of human rights, human decency and respect for the law."*

In the following viewpoint, author Bill Press argues that Guantanamo Bay, the American military prison on the island of Cuba, should be shut down. First, severe abuses and human rights violations have been documented, he claims; stories abound of inmates being tortured and humiliated by American guards. Secondly, hundreds of prisoners locked up at Guantanamo do not even belong there—many were simply swept up in raids following the Afghanistan War and have been sitting in the prison ever since. Finally, Press warns that the human rights abuses and violations of international law at Guantanamo Bay only serve to harpoon the United States' image as a fair and decent nation, which serves to recruit more terrorists to the cause of its destruction. For these reasons, Press urges leaders to close the military prison at Guantanamo Bay.

Bill Press, "Stop the Bleeding: Shut Down Guantanamo Bay," www.billpress.com, June 17, 2005. Reproduced by permission.

Bill Press is a TV and radio commentator, speaking on issues from education, to economics, to social issues and the environment. He currently hosts *The Bill Press Show*, a nationally syndicated radio talk show.

AS YOU READ, CONSIDER THE FOLLOWING QUESTIONS:
1. Why did officials think Guantanamo Bay was the perfect place to house suspected terrorists, according to the author?
2. In what way is Guantanamo Bay a "big black eye" on the face of the United States, in the author's opinion?
3. According to the Pentagon, what percentage of Guantanamo Bay inmates do not belong there?

Before you believe White House propaganda about the military prison at Guantanamo Bay serving as an essential front in the war on terror, consider the latest evidence.

Torture and Abuse at Guantanamo Bay

According to official prison logs, Mohammed al-Qahtani, a suspected terrorist from Saudi Arabia, was forcibly injected with three and half bags of fluid. He was stripped nude and made to get down on all fours and bark like a dog. He was forced to wear pictures of scantily clad women hung around his neck, then held down on the floor while a female soldier straddled his chest (a religious affront to devout Muslims). And when he told interrogators he had to relieve himself, they made him wet his pants.

News of Qahtani's treatment follows release of an e-mail from an FBI agent, sent to investigate conditions at Guantanamo Bay: "On a couple of occasions, I

> **FAST FACT**
>
> On June 10, 2006, three Guantanamo Bay detainees killed themselves in their cells. The Center for Constitutional Rights, which represents about 300 of the inmates, claimed the detainees' suicides were due to a belief they would never be tried justly.

entered interview rooms to find a detainee chained hand and foot in a fetal position to the floor, with no chair, food or water. Most times they urinated or defecated on themselves, and had been left there for 18–24 hours or more."

A Problem Installation from Day One

The U.S. Naval Station at Guantanamo Bay has been a problem installation from day one. It was created in 1898, at the conclusion of the Spanish-American War, when we seized Cuba from Spain. It is the only U.S. base today in a communist country, and the only one in a country that doesn't want us. Castro, in fact, refuses to cash the $4,000 annual rent check he receives from the United States.

Originally, detention centers at Guantanamo Bay were built to house Cuban and Haitian refugees caught trying to sneak into the United States. But in 2002, the Pentagon selected Gitmo [short for Guantanamo] as the perfect place to store suspected terrorists rounded up in Afghanistan. Why? Because it was totally controlled by the United States, yet located on foreign soil. Therefore, argued then-White House Counsel Alberto Gonzalez, American laws did not apply. There was no need to offer detainees any legal protection or even treat them as prisoners of war. They were called "enemy combatants" instead.

Flagrant Abuse of Human Rights and Law

The Supreme Court rejected that argument, but the Bush administration still refuses to budge. So today, Guantanamo Bay is a big black eye on the face of the United States, contradicting everything we supposedly stand for—in terms of human rights, human decency and respect for the law. No wonder Amnesty International has branded it "the gulag of our times." Some 550 prisoners have been held there for over three years with no charges filed, no chance to see a lawyer and no opportunity to defend themselves in a court of law. And many have been subjected to cruel, inhuman and degrading treatment.

Vice President Dick Cheney defends the administration's policies, telling Sean Hannity on Fox News: "The important thing here to understand is that the people that are in Guantanamo are bad people." He's dead wrong. Even the Pentagon admits that 40 percent of the original prison population didn't belong there in the first place. They weren't

There have been reports of prisoner abuse at the Pul-e-Charky detention center in Afghanistan and the Guantanamo Bay detention center in Cuba.

terrorists. They were innocent citizens of Afghanistan or, later, Iraq identified as al-Qaida sympathizers by bounty-hunting countrymen. So far, over 200 have been released. And in three years, not one Guantanamo prisoner has been charged with, let alone convicted of, terrorism.

Guantanamo Bay Helps the Terrorist Cause

Worse yet, stories from Guantanamo Bay now serve today as al-Qaida's best recruitment tools. Forget all the rhetoric about freedom. Show young Muslims the way we treat prisoners at Gitmo or Abu Ghraib and they're ready to sign up immediately—for the war against Americans.

Houston, we've got a problem, a serious image problem around the world. If we deny it, like Dick Cheney, or ignore it, like George W. Bush, it's only going to get worse. Instead, we must fix the problem, fast. As recommended by Democrats Joe Biden and Jimmy Carter and Republican Mel Martinez, it's time to close the military prison at Guantanamo, move all remaining prisoners to a military base on

American soil—and begin to follow international law governing prisoners of war.

To me, that's the most important consideration of all. Reread the evidence of prisoner abuse at Guantanamo Bay. Then ask yourself: Is this the way we would want American prisoners of war to be treated? If your answer is no, there's only one answer: Shut Gitmo down!

EVALUATING THE AUTHOR'S ARGUMENTS:

Bill Press claims that Guantanamo Bay inmates have been tortured and abused by U.S. guards. How might Michelle Malkin, author of the following viewpoint, respond to this claim?

The Military Prison at Guantanamo Bay Should Stay Open

Michelle Malkin

> *"Guantanamo Bay will not be the death of this country. The unseriousness and hypocrisy of the terrorist-abetting left is a far greater threat."*

In the following viewpoint, author Michelle Malkin rejects claims that Guantanamo Bay is the site of torture and abuse of military prisoners. Malkin argues that while there have been some instances of abuse, most have been exaggerated or completely made up by crafty inmates trained to lie and gain sympathy for their cause. In general, prisoners are treated well, says Malkin; they live in comfortable conditions, receive square meals, and even have their religious beliefs respected and accommodated. She concludes that America needs Guantanamo Bay to house dangerous prisoners from the war on terror: those who seek its closure do not have America's protection and best interests at heart.

Michelle Malkin is a nationally syndicated columnist and the author of *Invasion: How America Still Welcomes Terrorists, Criminals, and Other Foreign Menaces to Our Shores*.

AS YOU READ, CONSIDER THE FOLLOWING QUESTIONS:
  1. Why does Malkin believe that one detainee, who claims to have been "beaten up like a dog," is lying?
  2. In what ways are the religious beliefs and practices of Guantanamo Bay inmates respected, as described by Malkin?
  3. According to the author, what constitutes a far greater threat to America than Guantanamo Bay?

The mainstream media and international human-rights organizations have relentlessly portrayed the Guantanamo Bay detention facility as a depraved torture chamber operated by sadistic American military officials defiling Islam at every turn. It's the "gulag of our time," wails Amnesty International. It's the "anti-Statue of Liberty," bemoans *New York Times* columnist Tom Friedman.

Have there been abuses? Yes. But here is the rest of the story—the story the Islamists and their sympathizers don't want you to hear.

Exaggerated or Fabricated Abuses

According to recently released FBI documents, inaccurately heralded by civil liberties activists and military-bashers as irrefutable evidence of widespread "atrocities" at Gitmo [short for Guantanamo]:

A significant number of detainee complaints were either exaggerated or fabricated (no surprise given al Qaeda's explicit instructions to trainees to lie). One detainee who claimed to have been "beaten, spit upon and treated worse than a dog" could not provide not a single detail pertaining to mistreatment by U.S. military personnel. Another detainee claimed that guards were physically abusive, but admitted he hadn't seen it.

Another detainee disputed one of the now-globally infamous claims that American guards had mistreated the Koran. The detainee said riots resulted from claims a guard dropped the Koran. In actuality, the detainee said, a detainee dropped the Koran then

> **FAST FACT**
>
> On June 28, 2004, the Supreme Court ruled in *Hamdi v. Rumsfeld* that "illegal combatants" such as those held at Guantanamo Bay can be held without charges or trial.

blamed a guard. Other detainees who complained about abuse of the Koran admitted they had never personally witnessed any such thing, but one said he heard non-Muslim soldiers touched the Koran when searching it for contraband.

Conditions Are Acceptable For a Prison

In one case, Gitmo interrogators apologized to a detainee for interviewing him prior to the end of Ramadan.

Several detainees indicated they had not experienced any mistreatment. Others complained about lack of privacy, lack of bed sheets, being unwillingly photographed, the guards' use of profanity and bad food.

If this is unacceptable, "gulag"-style "torture," then every inmate in America is a victim of human-rights violations. (Oh, never mind, there are civil liberties Chicken Littles who actually believe that.)

Erik Saar, an army sergeant at Gitmo for six months and co-author of a negative, tell-all book titled "Inside the Wire," inadvertently provides us more firsthand details showing just how restrained, and sensitive to Islam—to a fault, I believe—the officials at the detention facility officials have been.

Amnesty International activists protest the prison holding people on suspicion of terrorist links in Guantanamo Bay, Cuba.

Inmates Are Respected and Well-Fed

Each detainee's cell has a sink installed low to the ground, "to make it easier for the detainees to wash their feet" before Muslim prayer, Mr. Saar reports. Detainees get "two hot halal, or religiously correct, meals" a day in addition to an MRE (meal ready to eat). Loudspeakers broadcast the Muslims' call to prayer five times day.

Every detainee gets a prayer mat, cap and Koran. Every cell has a stenciled arrow pointing toward Mecca. Moreover, Gitmo's library—yes, library—is stocked with Jihadi books. "I was surprised that we'd be making that concession to the religious zealotry of the terrorists," Mr. Saar admits. "It seemed to me that the camp command was helping to facilitate the terrorists' religious devotion." Mr. Saar notes that one FBI special agent involved in interrogations even grew a beard like the detainees "as a sort of show of respect for their faith."

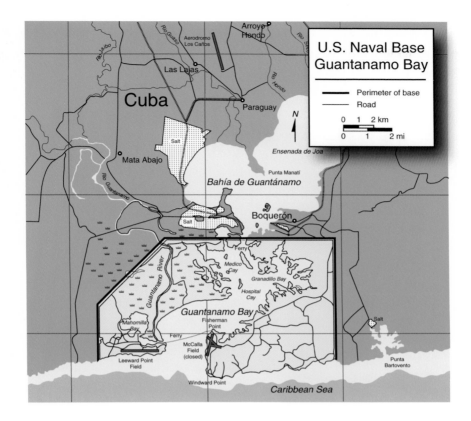

Treating Prisoners Like Prisoners and Enemies Like Enemies

Unreality-based liberals would have us believe America is systematically torturing innocent Muslims at Guantanamo Bay. Meanwhile, our own MPs [military police] have endured little-publicized abuse at the hands of manipulative, hatemongering enemy combatants. Detainees have spit on and hurled water, urine and feces on the MPs. Causing disturbances is a source of entertainment for detainees who, as Gen. Richard Myers notes, "would turn right around and try to slit our throats, slit our children's throats" if released.

The same unreality-based liberals whine about the Bush administration's failure to gather intelligence and prevent terrorism. Yet, these hysterical critics have no viable alternative to detention and interrogation—and there is no doubt they would be the first to lambaste the White House and Pentagon if a released detainee went on to commit an act of mass terrorism on American soil.

Guantanamo Bay will not be the death of this country. The unseriousness and hypocrisy of the terrorist-abetting left is a far greater threat.

EVALUATING THE AUTHOR'S ARGUMENTS:

Bill Press, author of the previous viewpoint, warns that Guantanamo Bay threatens to hurt America's image overseas and inspire terrorism against it. Michelle Malkin, on the other hand, believes that the greater threat to America's image is its willingness to be soft on those who deserve punishment and liberal citizens who hysterically exaggerate conditions at the prison. After reading both viewpoints, with which perspective do you agree? Explain your answer using evidence from the text.

The Use of International Prisons Helps Fight Terrorism

Condoleezza Rice

"Renditions take terrorists out of action, and save lives."

In the following viewpoint, Secretary of State Condoleezza Rice explains why the use of international prisons helps fight terrorism. Because terrorists are not loyal to any government, they often cannot be returned to a "home state" for processing. Furthermore, a legal process known as rendition makes it legal for nations to swap prisoners for detainment. This is why, in Rice's opinion, prisons such as Guantanamo Bay are lawful and necessary places to hold suspected terrorists until their link to terrorism can be fully determined. Rice assures Americans that the people held in international prisons are treated lawfully and respectfully, and believes these institutions are critical to keeping America safe from further terrorist attacks.

Condoleezza Rice was first the National Security Advisor and then the Secretary of State in the George W. Bush administration.

Condoleezza Rice, "Remarks at Andrews Air Force Base in Maryland," mauritius.usembassy.gov, December 5, 2005.

AS YOU READ, CONSIDER THE FOLLOWING QUESTIONS:
  1. What does the word "stateless" mean in the context of the viewpoint?
  2. Explain the process of rendition, as described by Rice.
  3. How long does international law allow a state to hold enemy combatants, according to Rice?

The United States and many other countries are waging a war against terrorism. For our country this war often takes the form of conventional military operations in places like Afghanistan and Iraq. Sometimes this is a political struggle, a war of ideas. It is a struggle waged also by our law enforcement agencies. Often we engage the enemy through the cooperation of our intelligence services with their foreign counterparts.

We must track down terrorists who seek refuge in areas where governments cannot take effective action, including where the terrorists cannot in practice be reached by the ordinary processes of law. In such places terrorists have planned the killings of thousands of innocents—in New York City or Nairobi, in Bali or London, in Madrid or Beslan, in Casablanca or Istanbul. Just two weeks ago [in November 2005] I visited a hotel ballroom in Amman, viewing the silent, shattered aftermath of one of those attacks.

The Issue of How to Handle Captured Terrorists

The United States, and those countries that share the commitment to defend their citizens, will use every lawful weapon to defeat these terrorists. Protecting citizens is the first and oldest duty of any government. Sometimes these efforts are misunderstood. I want to help all of you understand the hard choices involved, and some of the responsibilities that go with them.

One of the difficult issues in this new kind of conflict is what to do with captured individuals who we know or believe to be terrorists. The individuals come from many countries and are often captured far from their original homes. Among them are those who are effectively stateless, owing allegiance only to the extremist cause of transnational terrorism. Many are extremely dangerous. And some have information that may save lives, perhaps even thousands of lives.

Keeping local commerce booming and keeping suspected terrorists out of the loop are just a couple of the many uses for international prisons.

Unlawful Combatants Defy Traditional Definition

The captured terrorists of the 21st century do not fit easily into traditional systems of criminal or military justice, which were designed for different needs. We have had to adapt. Other governments are now also facing this challenge.

We consider the captured members of al Qaeda and its affiliates to be unlawful combatants who may be held, in accordance with the law of war, to keep them from killing innocents. We must treat them in accordance with our laws, which reflect the values of the American people. We must question them to gather potentially significant, life-saving, intelligence. We must bring terrorists to justice wherever possible.

Using Rendition—A Legal Procedure

For decades, the United States and other countries have used "renditions" to transport terrorist suspects from the country where they were captured to their home country or to other countries where they can be questioned, held, or brought to justice.

In some situations a terrorist suspect can be extradited according to traditional judicial procedures. But there have long been many other cases where, for some reason, the local government cannot detain or prosecute a suspect, and traditional extradition is not a good option. In those cases the local government can make the sovereign choice to cooperate in a rendition. Such renditions are permissible under international law and are consistent with the responsibilities of those governments to protect their citizens.

Taking Terrorists Out of Action

Rendition is a vital tool in combating transnational terrorism. Its use is not unique to the United States, or to the current administration. Last year, then Director of Central Intelligence George Tenet recalled that our earlier counterterrorism successes included "the rendition of many dozens of terrorists prior to September 11, 2001."

- Ramzi Youssef masterminded the 1993 bombing of the World Trade Center and plotted to blow up airliners over the Pacific Ocean, killing a Japanese airplane passenger in a test of one of his bombs. Once tracked down, a rendition brought him to the United States, where he now serves a life sentence.
- One of history's most infamous terrorists, best known as "Carlos the Jackal," had participated in murders in Europe and the Middle East. He was finally captured in Sudan in 1994. A rendition by the French government brought him to justice in France, where he is now imprisoned. Indeed, the European Commission of Human Rights rejected Carlos' claim that his rendition from Sudan was unlawful.

Renditions take terrorists out of action, and save lives.

The United States Treats All of Its Prisoners Lawfully

In conducting such renditions, it is the policy of the United States, and I presume of any other democracies who use this procedure, to comply with its laws and comply with its treaty obligations, including those under the Convention Against Torture. Torture is a term that is defined by law. We rely on law to govern our operations. The United States does not permit, tolerate, or condone torture under any circumstances. Moreover, in accordance with the policy of this administration:

- The United States has respected—and will continue to respect—the sovereignty of other countries.
- The United States does not transport, and has not transported, detainees from one country to another for the purpose of interrogation using torture.
- The United States does not use the airspace or airports of any country for the purpose of transporting a detainee to a country where he or she will be tortured.
- The United States has not transported anyone, and will not transport anyone, to a country when we believe he will be tortured. Where appropriate, the United States seeks assurances that transferred persons will not be tortured.

Military Prisoners Will Be Held to Prevent Terrorism

International law allows a state to detain enemy combatants for the duration of hostilities. Detainees may only be held for an extended period if the intelligence or other evidence against them has been carefully evaluated and supports a determination that detention is lawful. The U.S. does not seek to hold anyone for a period beyond what is necessary to evaluate the intelligence or other evidence against them, prevent further acts of terrorism, or hold them for legal proceedings.

With respect to detainees, the United States government complies with its Constitution, its laws, and its treaty obligations. Acts of physical or mental torture are expressly prohibited. The United States government does not authorize or condone torture of detainees. Torture, and conspiracy to commit torture, are crimes under U.S. law, wherever they may occur in the world.

Violations of these and other detention standards have been investigated and punished. There have been cases of unlawful treatment of detainees, such as the abuse of a detainee by an intelligence agency contractor in Afghanistan or the horrible mistreatment of some prisoners at Abu Ghraib that sickened us all and which arose under the different legal framework that applies to armed conflict in Iraq. In such cases the United States has vigorously investigated, and where appropriate, prosecuted and punished those responsible. Some individuals have already been sentenced to lengthy terms in prison; others have been demoted or reprimanded. . . .

Debating What Is Right

Debate in and among democracies is natural and healthy. I hope that debate also includes a healthy regard for the responsibilities of governments to protect their citizens.

Four years after 9/11, most of our populations are asking us if we are doing all we can to protect them. I know what it is like to face an inquiry into whether everything was done that could have been done. So now, before the next attack, we should all consider the hard choices that democratic governments must face. We can all best meet this danger if we work together.

EVALUATING THE AUTHOR'S ARGUMENTS:

Condoleezza Rice is a key player in the Bush Administration, which has since the 9/11 attacks become known for taking an aggressive and uncompromising stance towards terrorism even if it means international law. Does knowing her background influence the way you interpret her views? Explain why or why not.

The Use of International Prisons Is Illegal

Jennifer Van Bergen

"The CIA Gulag of detention camps spread around the globe violates numerous provisions of both domestic and international law."

In the following viewpoint, Jennifer Van Bergen explains why it is illegal for the U.S. to secretly detain enemy combatants in overseas prisons. Such detentions violate the Geneva Conventions, the international standard of legal behavior in war-time. Conduct by U.S. military police at Guantanamo Bay, such as the humiliation and degradation of inmates, is specifically prohibited by the Geneva Conventions, according to Van Bergen. Such conduct also violates the United States' own laws about war-time detentions. For these violations of international law, the author says U.S. officials, even President Bush whose signature appears on secret orders to set up overseas prisons for enemy combatants, can be held accountable.

Jennifer Van Bergen is a journalist with a law degree, and the author of *The Twilight of Democracy: The Bush Plan for America*. She writes frequently on civil liberties, human rights, and international law.

AS YOU READ, CONSIDER THE FOLLOWING QUESTIONS:
1. What are "black sites," as described by the author?
2. What does the word "gulag" mean, in the context of the viewpoint?
3. Who is protected by Common Article 3 (CA3) of the Geneva Conventions?

The *Washington Post* recently reported that there now exists a secret overseas network of CIA-run prisons—called "black sites." According to the *Post*, "several former and current intelligence officials and other U.S. government officials" claim the network was created in order to avoid U.S. laws that prohibit such detentions. But the law, it turns out, cannot be so easily avoided.

Out of Step with its Allies

A 2006 poll by the Program on International Policy Attitudes found that while the majority of Americans believe procedures at Guantanamo Bay and other overseas detention centers are legal, citizens in Britain, Germany, and Poland believe the U.S. has violated international law regarding its handling of enemy combatants.

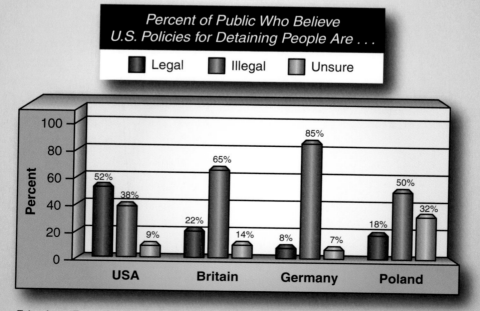

Percent of Public Who Believe
U.S. Policies for Detaining People Are . . .

■ Legal   ■ Illegal   ■ Unsure

USA: 52%, 38%, 9%
Britain: 22%, 65%, 14%
Germany: 8%, 85%, 7%
Poland: 18%, 50%, 32%

Taken from: "Europe Decries U.S. on Guantanamo Situation," Angus Reid Global Monitor: Polls & Research, July 18, 2006.

Secret Foreign Prisons Are Illegal

Indeed, such a detention system may violate both domestic and international laws. For this reason, it raises questions of legal liability, and accountability, not just for those who maintain these facilities, but also for those who ordered or sanctioned their creation.

As I explain below, secret overseas detentions by U.S. officials are barred by international law, by the extension of U.S. law to official conduct overseas, and by the domestic laws that incorporate or execute international treaties.

International Law on Detaining Combatants

Common Article 3 (CA3) of the 1949 Geneva Conventions, which has been described as "'a convention within a convention' to provide a general formula covering respect for intrinsic human values that would always be in force, without regard to the characterization the parties to a conflict might give it," protects any detainee under any circumstances. The denial of its protections is therefore a grave breach of Geneva and a war crime under the United States' War Crimes Act of 1996.

CA3 prohibits taking hostages, and it prohibits outrages upon personal dignity, including humiliating and degrading treatment. It also prohibits the passing of sentences and carrying out of executions without a previous judgment by a regularly constituted court affording all judicial guarantees.

Additionally, transfer of any person who is not a prisoner of war out of occupied territory is a grave breach of the Geneva Conventions, as well as a war crime. Deportation is also a crime against humanity under the Nuremberg Charter.

U.S. Detentions at Overseas Prisons are Unlawful

Enforced disappearances are also barred by international law, as are arbitrary detentions. According to Article 7 of the Declaration on the Protection of All Persons from Enforced Disappearances, adopted by the U.N. General Assembly in 1992, "no circumstances whatsoever" may justify enforced disappearances.

A U.N. Working Group on Arbitrary Detention declared that U.S. detentions without status determinations constitute arbitrary detentions in violation of the Third Geneva Convention. The Parliamentary

Assembly of the European Council resolved in 2003 that the detentions in Guantanamo, Afghanistan, and elsewhere were unlawful.

International law also bars incommunicado detention, even when it does not constitute "disappearance." The Restatement (Third) of Foreign Relations Law states that both disappearances and prolonged arbitrary detentions violate international law.

The Geneva Conventions provide that prisoners' whereabouts must be documented and made available to their family and governments, and that the International Committee of the Red Cross must have access to all detainees and places of detention—except where prevented by military necessity, but even then, only under exceptional and temporary circumstances.

The Geneva Convention also prohibits holding prisoners in "close confinement." Holding detainees "in dark, sometimes underground cells," according to the *Post*, is clearly prohibited.

Enemy Combatant Status

It could also be argued that prolonged incommunicado detention is inhumane and violates the International Covenant on Civil and Political

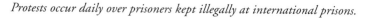

Protests occur daily over prisoners kept illegally at international prisons.

Rights, and the Convention Against Torture and Other Cruel, Inhuman or Degrading Treatment or Punishment. The U.S. reservations to the Torture Convention require compliance with the Eighth Amendment's prohibition of cruel and unusual punishment.

While authority exists for detaining enemy combatants during war, only a prisoner of war may be detained, and only for the duration hostilities, and a combatant may not be denied POW status without a status hearing, per the Third Geneva Convention.

Anyone not deemed an enemy combatant and protected as a POW is protected by the Fourth Geneva Convention as a civilian, and may not be detained without due process.

The U.S.'s Own Laws Against Unlawful Detentions

The 1996 War Crimes Act provides for severe criminal penalties for grave breaches of the Geneva and Hague Conventions, including Common Article 3.

But even where no violation of the Geneva or Hague Conventions is found, courts have held that the U.S. cannot excuse overseas conduct by claiming it was conducted in a foreign country under foreign official control, if the U.S. was involved in the conduct and if the conduct "shocks the conscience." Thus, in cases where the U.S. participates in unlawful detentions and interrogations of terrorist suspects by foreign officials, the U.S. may still be violating U.S. law, despite the foreign government's formally being the one that is holding the detainee.

U.S. courts have held that U.S. officials are responsible for conscience-shocking acts taking place on foreign soil or carried out by foreign officials if U.S. officials engaged or participated in a joint operation, if the involvement was such that foreign officials could be considered as agents of the U.S., or if the joint conduct was designed to evade constitutional protections. Although such doctrines have never been used to prosecute officials for their conduct, these cases may provide a framework to assist courts in determining liability.

U.S. Officials Can be Held Accountable

U.S. officials may incur liability for grave violations of international law under the 1996 War Crimes Act, and Geneva and the Nuremberg Charter exclude any form of immunity for war crimes. Obedience to orders is no defense to such charges, though it may mitigate the severity of punishment. Geneva Common Article 1 imposes the positive duty to respect and ensure respect for the Geneva Conventions in all circumstances on all parties.

Additionally, the doctrine of command responsibility requires that where a commander knows, or should have known, that his troops are committing war crimes and fails to prevent them, he is liable for their actions.

International Prisons are Illegal

According to *Newsweek*, President Bush signed a secret order authorizing the CIA to set up the black sites.

In conclusion, the CIA Gulag of detention camps spread around the globe violates numerous provisions of both domestic and international law. And the legal liability for these camps falls not just on CIA operatives, but on those Administration officials who have authorized or sanctioned these practices.

EVALUATING THE AUTHOR'S ARGUMENTS:

In the previous viewpoint, Secretary of State Condoleezza Rice argues that terrorists do not fall squarely into traditional systems or definitions of military or criminal justice. How do you think Jennifer Van Bergen would respond to the claim that international law does not apply to enemy combatants such as those held at Guantanamo Bay? Explain your answer using evidence from the text.

The United States Tortures Its Political Prisoners

Eliza Griswold

" 'They pulled our legs and we fell on our faces and they hit us with rifle butts. They walked on us like we were piano keys.' "

In the following viewpoint, author Eliza Griswold contends that the United States has tortured prisoners of the War on Terror. She discusses the stories of two men held in U.S. custody in Guantanamo Bay and other U.S. detention sites. Both men tell of being tortured, humiliated, and mistreated at the hands of U. S. forces. Furthermore, both men were held without trial, says Griswold, and were never charged with a crime; two things that are in violation of several international law treaties and condemned by the U.S. Supreme Court. Griswold concludes that the United States is grossly mistreating the prisoners it has taken in the war on terror.

Eliza Griswold is a Nieman Fellow at Harvard University. She has written a book of poetry and another article entitled "It's Not Easy Here in Katmandu" for *Harper's Magazine*, from which this viewpoint was taken.

AS YOU READ, CONSIDER THE FOLLOWING QUESTIONS:
1. How many political prisoners have died in U.S. custody since the beginning of the war on terror, as reported by Griswold?
2. Who is Abdullah al Noaimi, and was he associated with al Qaeda or the Taliban, according to the author?
3. Describe the treatment of Yemeni Abdulsalam by U.S. forces, as reported by Griswold.

Every year, the U.S. government sends Fidel Castro a check for $4,085 to pay the rent on forty-five square miles of Guantanamo Bay real estate. Castro, who has long wanted the United States to vacate the premises, refuses to cash the checks. The lease agreement, which dates from 1934, cannot be broken without the consent of both countries, and it is unlikely that ours will ever be given. We have, after all, a network of seven prison camps there, and we've just spent $30 million to open an eighth.

The Courts Call American Overseas Detention Facilities Illegal

The U.S. Supreme Court recently acknowledged, in *Hamdan v. Bush*, that holding a human being in such a facility, and subjecting him to torture, and denying him even those protections afforded POWs [prisoners of war], is in direct violation of Article Three of the Geneva Conventions. Yet there is no indication that this ruling will actually improve the lots of the 450 prisoners held at Guantanamo, let alone the 13,000 people currently "detained" in Iraq, the 500 or so in Afghanistan, and the unknown number (estimated to be about 100) at secret CIA "black sites" around the world. There is no indication that the ruling will at all alter the conditions under which, to date, 98 detainees have died (34 of these deaths are being investigated as homicides) and more than 600 U.S. personnel have been implicated in some form of abuse. President Bush maintained shortly after the decision that the Supreme Court had actually ruled in his favor. "They were silent on whether or not Guantanamo—whether or not we should have used Guantanamo," he said. "In other words, they accepted the use of Guantanamo, the decision I made.". . .

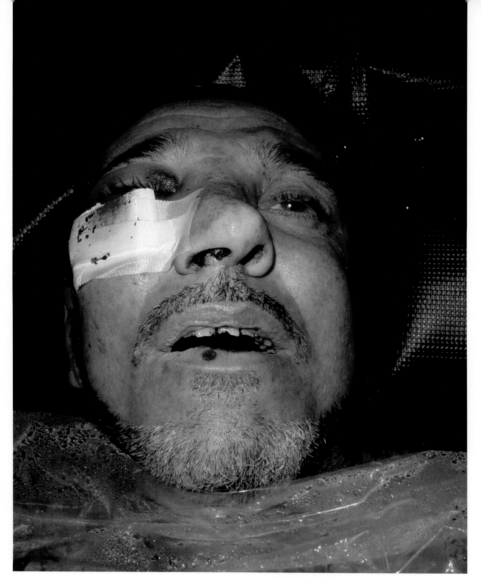

Incidents with inmates at Abu Ghraib prison put prison torture back in the forefront.

One Man's Nightmare

Last winter, twenty-four-year-old Abdullah al Noaimi returned home from more than four years of prison in Cuba to the tiny island kingdom of Bahrain. Abdullah lives in Bahrain's wealthiest suburb, Riffa, near a Starbucks and across the street from King Hot Dog, where those close to the royal family have homes. One evening, several weeks after he had returned home, Tina and I knocked on the al Noaimis' steel gate. A servant led us past a Nautilus machine and swimming pool to

FBI agents, Red Cross inspectors, and numerous released detainees (including those with no known connection to terrorism) are just a few of those who have claimed that Guantanamo Bay detainees have been tortured, sleep-deprived, given truth serum drugs, or beaten. Some human rights groups consider indefinite detention to be torture in and of itself.

where Abdullah sat in a marble-floored reception room with his mother, his aunt, and two of his sisters. His father works for King Hamad bin Isa al Khalifa. His grandmother was a princess. When Abdullah's mother saw Tina, she hugged her and started to cry. . . .

There are three kinds of detainees: high-ranking Al Qaeda suspects; men who are not necessarily accused of anything but may have intelligence value; and those, like Abdullah, who were supposedly rounded up on the battlefield, fighting against Coalition troops. Any of these may be designated enemy combatants. Abdullah was accused of traveling to Afghanistan with the intention of fighting jihad, an accusation he denies. Like 95 percent of the detainees at Guantanamo, Abdullah wasn't arrested by Americans. Instead, he was abducted and sold by Pashtun tribesmen to Pakistani security forces. At the time of his arrest, in late 2001, there seemed to be a bounty on every Arab's head, and fliers promising "wealth and power beyond your dreams" were dropping, as Defense Secretary Donald Rumsfeld said, "like snowflakes in December in Chicago." The Pakistanis piled Abdullah and others into the back of a truck. "They blindfolded and cuffed us," he said. "I shouted at them, 'You monsters, you don't even know what Islam is.' "

Passed From Country to Country

Over the next two weeks, Abdullah was taken to a series of prisons in Pakistan's tribal areas, along the Afghan border, and eventually to a large prison at Kohat. The prison at Kohat and another at Alizai are significant because, according to Human Rights First, both are suspected of being proxy detention centers, where detainees are held by third-party countries—Jordan, Egypt, Morocco, and Syria among

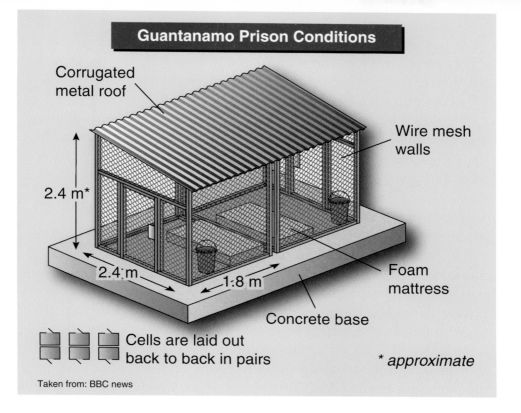

Guantanamo Prison Conditions

Corrugated metal roof

Wire mesh walls

2.4 m*

2.4 m

1.8 m

Foam mattress

Concrete base

Cells are laid out back to back in pairs

* approximate

Taken from: BBC news

them—allowing the United States to deny culpability for abuses committed on its behalf. After several weeks there, Abdullah heard that he and other prisoners were going to be handed over to the Americans.

"When I was told I was going to be taken to the Americans, I was relieved. Please, take me to an American prison," he said. Under American justice, he believed, innocent men like him were sure to be released. That was more than four years ago. . . .

Tied Like a Package

During his first interrogation by the Americans, Abdullah realized that things were not as he'd expected. An American man and woman, who were not wearing uniforms, became furious when he told them he'd visited the States numerous times and had even attended Old Dominion. Abdullah told them he was nineteen; they decided he was thirty. He remembers being "tied like a package, covered with a white cloth" on his journey to Afghanistan. "It was very cold and quiet," he said. "There were thirty of us tied together." Half of these men were then taken into a tent and heard the sound of triggers being cocked.

"They pulled our legs and we fell on our faces and they hit us with rifle butts. They walked on us like we were piano keys."

I asked him what happened next.

He laid his head back against the couch. "They cut off my clothes, and men and women were there. . . ." He paused and looked at the floor. "I prefer to skip this part," he said. "I don't want anyone to know what happened to me.". . .

Cuffed, Hooded, and Gagged

After several days of interrogation in Cairo, [another prisoner in the war on terror, a Yemeni man named] Abdulsalam was loaded into a minibus by the Egyptian intelligence officers and taken to the airport. On the runway a group of ski-masked men waited in front of a private plane. According to flight plans obtained by British journalist Stephen Grey, the day after Abdulsalam disappeared a Gulfstream V, tail-number N379P, left Dulles airport in the early morning, landed in Athens, and then continued on to Cairo, landing the day before the Egyptians handed Abdulsalam over to the hooded soldiers. The soldiers cut off his suit, stripped him naked, and searched him. They dressed him in a blue jumpsuit and blindfolded him. He was loaded onto the plane, where he was waist-cuffed, hooded, and gagged. That night, at 11:01, the CIA plane left Cairo for Kabul. This plane was and is owned by Premiere Executive Transport Services, a CIA front company. Its tail number has since been changed at least three times.

Abdulsalam was imprisoned in Afghanistan for two years, first in a prison the detainees call the "dark prison," because prisoners there are held in total darkness. At the dark prison, Abdulsalam was hung from the wall by chains. As he would eventually explain to his lawyer, "In the prison of darkness, they made up stories, and I said I'll thumbprint anything—just let me sleep and give me clothes. I was naked." One hand was cuffed to the wall at all times, which made it hard to sleep or to use the toilet. "It sounds bizarre at first," his lawyer Marc Falkoff told me. "But look at the leaked interrogation logs. They do weird, surreal things designed to disorient and humiliate the men."

Treatment Meant to Disorient and Humiliate

Meanwhile, Abdulsalam's family had no idea where he had gone. The Egyptian Embassy in Yemen said that he'd been sent "on a special plane" to Baku, Azerbaijan. Finally, they received a letter smuggled out of Afghanistan by another prisoner. Abdulsalam wrote that after almost two years in Afghanistan he was taken to the U.S. base at Bagram. In 2002, two Afghan men were killed there after being chained and hung from the ceiling and brutally beaten. According to a coroner's testimony, one of the deceased, a taxi driver named Dilawar, had his legs "pulpified." If he'd lived, both of them would have required amputation. Like many detainees, Abdulsalam prefers not to talk about his time at Bagram, because, he says, the "wounds are too bad."

EVALUATING THE AUTHOR'S ARGUMENTS:

Eliza Griswold focuses on the stories of two prisoners, letting them tell their stories in their own words. Did you find this method of writing to be particularly powerful or compelling? Or, did you find the focus on the two men to be too narrow to convince you that the United States routinely tortures its prisoners? Explain which position resonates with you.

The United States Does Not Torture Its Political Prisoners

Byron York

"It appears the administration is simply not guilty of the misconduct of which it has been accused."

In the following viewpoint, author Byron York argues that U.S. troops treat political prisoners humanely and in accordance with U.S. and international law. He describes several review processes that have made sure interrogation techniques used at Guantanamo Bay detention facility and elsewhere are humane. U.S. military leaders are committed to upholding American values in their military prisons, he contends, concluding that accusations of torture in such facilities are farfetched and fabricated. The overwhelming majority of military personnel treat prisoners professionally and appropriately, in his opinion.

Byron York is a journalist and the White House correspondent for the *National Review*, from which this viewpoint was taken.

AS YOU READ, CONSIDER THE FOLLOWING QUESTIONS:
  1. Who is Mohamed al-Kahtani, as described by York?
  2. Explain the tactic of dietary manipulation, as described by the author.
  3. According to the author, what is the "dirty little secret" of U.S. troops that handle prisoners in the war on terror?

On Sunday, June 20, [2004] at the U.S. detention facility in Guantanamo Bay, Cuba, the lunch menu for suspected al-Qaeda, Taliban, and other prisoners in the War on Terror was as follows: whole-wheat pita bread, stewed tomatoes, long-grain brown rice, chickpeas, dates, yogurt, and tea. For dinner, the suspected terrorists were served green beans, carrots, chicken and noodles, whole-wheat bread, fresh fruit, and tea. For both meals, as for all others served at what is known as Camp Delta, U.S. forces took care to make sure the food served to Muslim prisoners was prepared in accordance with halal dietary requirements. Detainees "receive three culturally appropriate meals each day," one official told *National Review*, and another officer e-mailed from Guantanamo to say, "I can reassure you that we are definitely attuned to the cultural dietary needs of the detainees. Nothing that is not appropriate is ever given to them to eat or drink."

Such measures, along with many others concerning the prisoners' daily lives, suggest that the American military is going to great lengths to ensure that detainees, a number of them jihadists captured on the battlefield in Afghanistan, are treated humanely.

False Accusations about Torture and Abuse

Yet in recent days the Bush administration has found itself facing accusations that it permits the "torture" of prisoners in the War on Terror. Critics in Congress and the press have suggested that the administration has not only condoned torture, but has used illegal methods of interrogation on detainees. . . .

Amid all the condemnations, a few questions remained largely unasked. What did those legal memos actually say about torture? How does the U.S. military treat its prisoners? Have any been tortured? A look at the administration's legal thinking, and interviews with those

U.S. Treats Detainees Fairly

A 2005 study of attitudes of prisoner treatment at Guantanamo Bay, Cuba, found that most Americans believe the detainees are treated fairly or better than they deserve.

Treatment of Prisoners at Guantanamo Bay

Unfair	20%
Better than they deserve	36%
About right	34%

Taken from: Rasmussen Reports, June 20–21, 2005.

involved in making its policies, suggest the answers come out in the administration's favor. Although such answers are less sexy than headlines about torture, it appears the administration is simply not guilty of the misconduct of which it has been accused.

An Exhaustive Review to Make Sure Tactics Are Not Torture

When the U.S. began shipping detainees to Guantanamo, the only rules that applied to interrogations were those found in Field Manual 34-52, an old publication that had guided American military interrogations for years. The manual listed 17 techniques that interrogators could use, such as incentives, removal of incentives, rapid-fire questions, and silence. Those guidelines governed all interrogations until December 2002.

By then, the military had been having problems with what one Pentagon source calls a "high-value detainee" who had al-Qaeda connections and who "we thought had some very specific information about future planned attacks on America." Officials will not name him publicly, but he has been identified in the press as Mohamed al-Kahtani, thought to be the intended "20th hijacker." "He was resisting these kinds of techniques," says the source. "We know that they [al-Qaeda] train to resist these things."

Al-Kahtani's resistance led to an extensive review of interrogation procedures. The reviewers went up and down the chain of command, and in the end came up with a new list of procedures. That list was divided into three tiers. The first tier involved most of the techniques that had been in the old field manual, plus a few new ones, "like yelling at a detainee, but not in his ear, and not to cause pain," says the Pentagon source.

Consulting to Approve of Treatment

The second tier involved strategies such as removing "comfort items," including toothpaste and other sundries. The third tier comprised just one technique: Officials will not give all the details, but it appears to have involved "non-injurious contact"—what the source calls "light pushing."

The new three-tier system had been in place for just a month when some military officials at Guantanamo raised concerns about its appropriateness and effectiveness. At that point, defense secretary Donald Rumsfeld convened a large working group to come up with yet another set of interrogation guidelines. The group included people from all disciplines in the military, including lawyers who opposed virtually all interrogation techniques.

An extensive debate took place, and the work went on for more than a year. Finally, in April 2003, the Pentagon approved a new set of interrogation methods that are still in effect today. The new set included 24 techniques—the 17 from the old field manual, plus seven new ones.

"We're Not Really Doing Very Much to Them"

The new methods included "dietary manipulation," which means a change in the detainee's daily rations. "It's not a reduction in caloric intake, and it's intended to provide the same level of nutrition, but perhaps just not as palatable," says the source. In practice, it has meant taking away a prisoner's hot meals and giving him instead a military MRE [meal ready to eat], the standard field ration for American troops. Other techniques included shaving off a detainee's beard (something the September 11 hijackers did for themselves, in order not to attract attention) and "change of scenery," such as taking a detainee to a smaller interrogation room than the one to which he had become accustomed.

Four of the 24 techniques required the approval of the secretary of defense himself. They were "attacking or insulting the ego of a detainee"; using a "team consisting of a friendly and harsh interrogator"; the reward or removal of significant incentives; and "isolation." Officials are quick to point out that "isolation" does not mean "solitary confinement." "It's removing him from his peer group, not removing him from all human contact," says the Pentagon source. Officials also stress that every interrogation is conducted only after an interrogation plan is written and approved in advance.

In total, what seems remarkable about the interrogation guidelines is, for the most part, how mild they are. In many ways, even the most recalcitrant detainee receives better treatment (and food) than many U.S. troops in the field (or in training). "The dirty little secret here is not how bad these guys are being treated," says the source. "The dirty little secret is we're not really doing very much to them."

Staying Loyal to American Values

On June 17, Rumsfeld faced the Pentagon press corps to answer a long series of questions about torture. . . . . Gathering his thoughts, Rumsfeld continued, "I have not seen anything that suggests that a senior civilian or military official of the United States of America . . . could be characterized as ordering or authorizing or permitting torture or acts that are inconsistent with our international treaty obligations or our laws or our values as a country."

What Rumsfeld did not mention—because it was classified at the time—was that for more than two years he and the entire American

Members of the Afghan nomadic Kuchi tribe detained at the U.S. prison in Guantanamo Bay, Cuba are prime examples of how the U.S. does not torture suspected terrorists in their prisons.

government have operated under a February 7, 2002, directive from President Bush that declared, "Our values as a nation, values that we share with many nations in the world, call for us to treat detainees humanely, including those who are not legally entitled to such treatment. As a matter of policy, the U.S. armed forces shall continue to treat detainees humanely, and to the extent appropriate and consistent with military necessity, in a manner consistent with the principles of Geneva."

U.S. Troops Treat Prisoners Humanely

America's military men and women seem to have taken that directive quite seriously. For example, while the prosecutions of soldiers involved in the Abu Ghraib abuses are well known, it is not as well known that the Pentagon has been quite tough—some would say too tough—on Americans who have run into trouble with terrorist detainees at Guantanamo. In one instance, according to military officials, a prisoner threw a cup of urine at a guard, who retaliated by throwing some Pine-Sol cleaner at the prisoner. In another case, a detainee spit on a guard, who then turned a water hose on him. In both cases, sources say, it was the guards, and not the detainees, who were disciplined.

That kind of story doesn't receive much notice in the ongoing uproar about torture. But in the end, such instances seem to show an administration determined to treat prisoners humanely—no matter what its critics say.

EVALUATING THE AUTHORS' ARGUMENTS:

Byron York begins his essay by describing in detail the lunch and dinner menu of prisoners at the Guantanamo Bay detention facility. Why do you think he chose to open his essay in this way? What point is he trying to make about life in the prison?

Facts About Prisons

Editor's note: These facts can be used in reports or papers to reinforce or add credibility when making important points or claims.

Prisons in America:

According to the International Centre for Prison Studies:
- There are 2,193,798 inmates in America's prison system.
  - 1,259,905 of these inmates are incarcerated in state prisons.
  - 747,529 are incarcerated in local jails.
  - 179,220 are incarcerated in federal prisons.
  - 7,144 are incarcerated in non-secure privately operated facilities.
  - 96,655 are incarcerated in juvenile facilities.
  - 1,745 are incarcerated in jails under Native American jurisdiction Indian country.
  - 10,104 are incarcerated in immigration facilities.
  - and 2,322 are incarcerated in military facilities.

As of 2005:
- There are 5,069 prison facilities or institutions in the United States.
- America's prisons operate at over-capacity. The official capacity of the U.S. prison system is 2,039,370, yet there are 2,193,798 inmates in custody.
- In total, U.S. prisons operate at 107.6% capacity. Local jails operate at 94.7% capacity; state prisons operate at 111% capacity; and federal prisons operate at 150.1% capacity,
- The U.S. prison population has steadily increased over the last decade:
  - in 1992 the population was 1,295,150
  - in 1995 the population was 1,585,586
  - in 1998 the population was 1,816,931
  - in 2001 the population was 1,961,247
  - in 2004 the population was 2,135,335
  - in 2005 the population was 2,193,798
- There are approximately 6.9 million Americans incarcerated or

on probation or parole, an increase of more than 275 percent since 1980.

- In 2004 over 600,000 inmates were released from prisons.
- The incarceration of an inmate costs taxpayers approximately $22,000 per year.
- In California, 50 inmates die each year as a result of lack of adequate medical care.

Facts About Inmates in America

According to the Bureau of Justice Statistics:
- 91.1% of prison inmates are male.
- Females comprise 8.9% of the prison population.
- Juveniles comprise 0.4% of the prison population.
- Foreign prisoners account for 6.4% of the prison population.
- As of 2005, there were 107,518 women in state or federal prisons.
- As of 2006 there were 3,145 black male sentenced prison inmates per 100,000 black males in the United States, compared to 1,244 Hispanic male inmates per 100,000 Hispanic males and 471 white male inmates per 100,000 white males.
- Black males have a 32% chance of serving time in prison at some point in their lives; Hispanic males have a 17% chance; white males have a 6% chance.
- Violent criminals make up 52% of all inmates; those incarcerated for property crimes 21%; for drug offenses, 20%, and for public-order violations, 7%.

According to the Bureau of Justice Statistics Prisoners in 2005 Bulletin:

In 2005, the states with the highest prison populations were:
- Federal 187,618
- California 170,676
- Texas 169,003
- Florida 89,768
- New York 62,743

The states with the lowest prison populations were:
- North Dakota 1,385
- Maine 2,023

- Wyoming 2,047
- Vermont 2,078
- New Hampshire 2,530

The states with the highest prisoner populations compared to state population were:
- Louisiana 797 per 100,000 residents
- Texas 691
- Mississippi 660
- Oklahoma 652
- Alabama 591

The states with the lowest prisoner populations compared to state population were:
- Maine 144
- Minnesota 180
- Rhode Island 189
- New Hampshire 192
- North Dakota 208

Prisons Around the World

According to the International Centre for Prison Studies 2005 figures:
- Over 9 million people are held in penal institutions throughout the world. Almost half of these are in the United States (2,193,798), China (1,548,498) or Russia (885,666).
- The United States has the highest prison population rate in the world. As of 2005 it was 737 inmates per 100,000 people.
- French Guiana/Guyane is next with an incarceration rate of 630; Russia follows with a rate of 524; the come St. Kitts and Nevis and the Virgin Islands, with rates of 604 and 549 respectively.
- The nations with the next highest rates of incarceration are Cuba (531 per 100,000), Belize (505 per 100,000), Turkmenistan (489), Palau (478), Bermuda (464), the Virgin Islands (464), and the Bahamas (462).
- The nations with the highest percentage of female inmates are:
  - The Maldives (21.6 percent of the prison population)
  - Monaco (20.6%)
  - Hong Kong (China) (20.2%)

- Myanmar (formerly Burma) (17.8%)
- Thailand (16.9%)
- Kuwait (14.9%)
- Vietnam (12.4%)
- United Arab Emirates (11.4%)
- Singapore (11%)
- Ecuador (10.7 %)

Glossary

Enemy combatants: the term given to prisoners of the war on terror. The term "prisoners of war" as described under the Geneva Conventions, was deemed inappropriate for those who fight not under a national army but on behalf of a terrorist group. As such, they are not afforded protections under the Geneva Conventions.

Geneva Conventions: a set of rules for war and treatment of prisoners that were widely adopted after World War II. For more than half a century they have been regarded as a comprehensive guide for undertaking global conflict.

Guantanamo Bay: the U.S. military base in Cuba where detainees from the war on terror are being held.

Gulag: a prison or detention camp, usually for political prisoners.

Incarceration: imprisonment.

Juvenile offender: An offender too young to be tried as an adult. The age at which a person can be tried as an adult varies between states, but is usually seventeen or eighteen. Juvenile offenders are not allowed to be housed in a regular prison facility; instead they must be placed in a juvenile correction center.

Mandatory minimum sentencing laws: a set of laws that were enacted in the 1980s to standardize sentences around the country. Mandatory minimum sentencing laws require a set amount of prison time for specific crimes, no matter the specifics of the case. They prevent judges from considering particular circumstances of each case that might result in less jail time, but also ensure that criminals around the country will serve equal times in prison for the same crime.

Prisoners of War: as defined by the Geneva Conventions, soldiers, meaning those who wear the uniform of their nation, have a rank and a superior, fight openly, and avoid violence against civilians.

Recidivism: repeated or habitual criminal relapse; the tendency to re-commit a crime.

Rehabilitation: the process of reforming a person.

Three-strikes laws: laws that require a 25 years-to-life sentence for criminals for their third conviction. Based on the idea of "three strikes and you're out," these laws sometimes end up imposing harsh sentences for minor crimes—but because it is a third conviction, the criminal is heavily penalized.

Organizations to Contact

The editors have compiled the following list of organizations concerned with the issues debated in this book. The descriptions are derived from materials provided by the organizations. All have publications or information available for interested readers. The list was compiled on the date of publication of the present volume; the information provided here may change. Be aware that many organizations take several weeks or longer to respond to inquiries, so allow as much time as possible.

American Civil Liberties Union (ACLU)

125 Broad St., 18th Floor,
New York, NY 10004-2400
(888) 567-ACLU
e-mail: aclu@aclu.org · Web site: www.aclu.org
Founded in 1920, the ACLU is a national organization that works to defend civil liberties in the United States. It publishes various materials on the Bill of Rights, including regular in-depth reports, the newsletter *Civil Liberties*, and a set of handbooks on individual rights.

American Civil Liberties Union (ACLU)
National Prison Project

1875 Connecticut Ave. NW, Suite 410, Washington, DC 20009
(202) 234-4830 · fax: (202) 234-4890
e-mail: aclu@aclu.org · Web site: www.aclu.org/prison/index.html
Formed in 1972, the project serves as a national resource center and litigates cases to strengthen and protect adult and juvenile offenders' Eighth Amendment rights. It opposes electronic monitoring of offenders and the privatization of prisons. The project publishes the quarterly *National Prison Project Journal* and various booklets.

Amnesty International (AI)

322 8th Avenue
New York, NY 10001
(212) 807-8400 · fax: (212) 463 9193
e-mail: admin-us@aiusa.org · Web site: www.amnesty.org
Made up of over 1.8 million members in over 150 countries, AI is dedicated to promoting human rights worldwide. Since its inception in 1961, the organization has focused much of its effort on the eradication of torture. AI maintains an extremely active news Web site, distributes a large annual report on the state of human rights in every country on Earth (as well as numerous special reports on specific human rights issues), and publishes *The Wire*, the monthly magazine of AI.

The Brookings Institution

1775 Massachusetts Ave. NW, Washington, DC 20036
(202) 797-6000 · fax: (202) 797-6004
e-mail: brookinfo@brook.edu · Web site: www.brookings.org
The institution, founded in 1927, is a think tank that conducts research and education in foreign policy, economics, government, and the social sciences. In 2001 it began America's Response to Terrorism, a project that provides briefings and analysis to the public and which is featured on the center's Web site. Other publications include the quarterly *Brookings Review,* periodic *Policy Briefs,* and books including *Terrorism and U.S. Foreign Policy.*

Center for Alternative Sentencing and Employment Services (CASES)

346 Broadway, 8th Fl., New York, NY 10013
(212) 732-0076 · fax: (212) 571-0292
e-mail: info@cases.org · Web site: www.cases.org
CASES seeks to end what it views as the overuse of incarceration as a response to crime. It operates two alternative-sentencing programs in New York City: the Court Employment Project, which provides intensive supervision and services for felony offenders, and the Community Service Sentencing Project, which works with repeat misdemeanor offenders. The center advocates in court for such offenders' admission into its programs. CASES publishes various program brochures.

Corrections Connection

159 Burgin Parkway, Quincy MA 02169
(617) 471-4445 · fax: (617) 770-3339
e-mail: editor@corrections.com · Web site: www.corrections.com
The Corrections Connection is committed to improving national and international correctional policy and to promoting the professional development of those working in the field of corrections. It offers a variety of books and correspondence courses on corrections and criminal justice.

European Committee for the Prevention of Torture and Inhuman or Degrading Treatment or Punishment (CPT)

Human Rights Building
Council of Europe
F-67075 Strasbourg Cedex
France
phone: +33 (3) 8841 3939 · fax: +33 (3) 8841 2772
e-mail: cptdoc@coe.int · Web site: www.cpt.coe.int
The CPT originated with the 1987 passage of the European Convention for the Prevention of Torture and Inhuman or Degrading Treatment or Punishment, an international treaty ratified by 45 members of the European Council. The CPT performs site visits in participating countries to ensure that no torture or other inhuman treatment is taking place. It maintains a large online database detailing torture reports and site visits and publishes numerous reports, standards, and reference documents pertaining to torture.

Families Against Mandatory Minimums (FAMM)

1612 K St. NW, Suite 1400, Washington, DC 20006
(202) 822-6700 · fax: (202) 822-6704
e-mail: famm@famm.org · Web site: www.famm.org
FAMM is an educational organization that works to repeal mandatory minimum sentences. It provides legislators, the public, and the media with information on and analyses of minimum-sentencing laws. FAMM publishes the quarterly newsletter *FAMM-gram*.

John Howard Society (JHS)

809 Blackburn Mews
Kingston, ON
Canada K7P 2N6
(613) 384-6272 · fax: (613) 384-1847
e-mail: national@johnhoward.ca · Web site: www.johnhoward.ca
The John Howard Society of Canada advocates reform in the criminal justice system and monitors governmental policy to ensure fair and compassionate treatment of prisoners. It views imprisonment as a last resort option. The organization provides education to the community, support services to at-risk youth, and rehabilitation programs to former inmates. Its publications include the booklet *Literacy and the Courts: Protecting the Right to Understand.*

Human Rights Watch (HRW)

350 Fifth Avenue, 34th Floor
New York, NY 10118-3299
(212) 290-4700 · fax: (212) 736-1300
e-mail: hrwnyc@hrw.org · Web site: www.hrw.org
In 1988, several large regional organizations dedicated to promoting human rights merged to form HRW, a global watchdog group. HRW publishes numerous books, policy papers, and special reports (including a comprehensive annual report), sponsors an annual film festival on human rights issues, and files lawsuits on behalf of those whose rights are violated.

International Committee of the Red Cross (ICRC)

Washington, D.C. Regional Delegation
2100 Pennsylvania Avenue NW, Suite 545
Washington, DC 20037
(202) 293-9430 · fax: (202) 293-9431
e-mail: washington.was@icrc.org · Web site: www.icrc.org
Founded in 1863, the ICRC is one of the few organizations to have won the Nobel Peace Prize (and did so on three occasions: in 1917, 1944, and 1963). It was the ICRC that led to the creation of the Geneva Conventions on the treatment of prisoners of war, the wounded, and medical personnel, among others. Today, the ICRC continues its mission by investigating reports of human rights viola-

tions, assisting in disaster relief, and working on behalf of those who are wounded or imprisoned in wartime.

National Center for Policy Analysis (NCPA)

12770 Coit Rd., Suite 800
Dallas, TX 75251-1339
(972) 386-6272 · fax: (972) 386-0924
e-mail: publications@ncpa.org · Web site: www.ncpa.org
NCPA is a nonprofit public policy research institute. It advocates more stringent prison sentences, the abolishment of parole, and restitution for crimes. Publications include the policy reports "Why Expected Punishment Deters Crime," "Parolees Return to Crime," and "Restitution Works for Juveniles."

National Center on Institutions and Alternatives (NCIA)

7222 Ambassador Road/Baltimore, MD 21244
(410) 265-1490 · Web site: www.ncianet.org/
NCIA is a criminal justice foundation that encourages community-based alternatives to prison that are more effective in providing education, training, and personal skills required for the rehabilitation of nonviolent offenders. The center advocates doubling "good conduct" credit for the early release of nonviolent first-time offenders in the federal system to make room for violent offenders. NCIA publishes books, reports, and the periodic newsletters *Criminal Defense Update* and *Jail Suicide/Mental Health Update*.

National Crime Prevention Council (NCPC)

1000 Connecticut Avenue, NW
13th Floor
Washington, DC 20036
(202)466-6272 · fax: (202)296-1356
e-mail: besafe@ncpc.org · Web site: www.ncpc.org
The NCPC provides training and technical assistance to groups and individuals interested in crime prevention. It advocates job training and recreation programs as a means to reduce crime and violence. The council, which sponsors the Take a Bite Out of Crime campaign, publishes the newsletter *Catalyst* ten times a year.

National Criminal Justice Reference Service (NCJRS)
U.S. Department of Justice
PO Box 6000, Rockville, MD 20849-6000
(800) 851-3420 · fax: (301) 519-5212
Web site: www.ncjrs.org
The National Criminal Justice Reference Service is one of the most extensive sources of information on criminal justice in the world. Provides topical searches and reading lists on many areas of criminal justice, including the death penalty. It publishes an annual report on capital punishment.

Prison Fellowship Ministries (PFM)
44180 Riverside Parkway
Lansdowne, VA 20176
(877)478-0100
Web site: www.prisonfellowship.org
Prison Fellowship Ministries encourages Christians to work in prisons and to assist communities in ministering to prisoners, ex-offenders, and their families. It works toward establishing a fair and effective criminal justice system and trains volunteers for in-prison ministries. Publications include the monthly *Jubilee* newsletter, the quarterly *Justice Report*, and numerous books, including *Born Again* and *Life Sentence*.

The Sentencing Project
514 Tenth Street, NW
Suite 1000
Washington DC 20004
(202)628-0871 · fax: (202)628-1091
e-mail: staff@sentencingproiect.org · Web site: www.sentencing project.org
The project seeks to provide public defenders and other public officials with information on establishing and improving alternative sentencing programs that provide convicted persons with positive and constructive options to incarceration. It promotes increased public understanding of the sentencing process and alternative sentencing programs. It publishes the reports "Americans Behind Bars: A Comparison of

International Rates of Incarceration" and "Young Black Men and the Criminal Justice System: A Growing National Problem."

U.S. Department of Justice
Federal Bureau of Prisons

320 First St. NW, Washington, DC 20534
e-mail: info@bop.gov · Web site: www.bop.gov/

The Federal Bureau of Prisons works to protect society by confining offenders in the controlled environments of prison and community-based facilities. It believes in providing work and other self-improvement opportunities within these facilities to assist offenders in becoming law-abiding citizens. The bureau publishes the book *The State of the Bureau.*

United States Naval Base at Guantanamo Bay, Cuba

PSC 1005 Box 25
FPO AE 09593

The U.S. Naval Base at Guantanamo Bay hosts hundreds of accused Taliban and al Qaeda fighters imprisoned during the Afghanistan War of 2001. Human rights groups argue that these detainees have been denied access to the U.S. criminal justice system and subjected to "stress and duress" interrogation techniques. In *Rasul v. Bush* (2004), the U.S. Supreme Court sided with the detainees and ruled that they have the right to challenge their status in U.S. civilian courts.

FOR FURTHER READING

Books

Demico Boothe, *Why Are So Many Black Men In Prison? A Comprehensive Account Of How And Why The Prison Industry Has Become A Predatory Entity In The Lives Of African-American Men.* Memphis, TN: Full Surface Publishing, 2007.

Jamuna Carroll, ed., *Writing the Critical Essay Prisons: An Opposing Viewpoints* Guide. Farmington Hills, MI: Greenhaven Press, 2006.

Alan Eisner, *Gates of Injustice: The Crisis of America's Prisons.* Princeton, NJ: Prentice Hall, 2004.

Joseph Margulies, *Guantanamo and the Abuse of Presidential Power.* New York: Simon & Schuster, 2007.

David L. Myers, *Boys Among Men: Trying and Sentencing Juveniles as Adults.* Westport, CT: Praeger, 2005.

T. J. Parsell, *Fish: A Memoir of a Boy in a Man's Prison.* New York: Carroll & Graf, 2006.

Jocyelyn M. Pollock, *Prisons and Prison Life: Costs and Consequences.* Los Angeles: Roxbury, 2004.

Prisons Foundation, *Prisons Almanac* 2005. Washington, DC: Prisons Foundation, 2005.

Jeffrey Reiman, *Rich Get Richer and The Poor Get Prison.* Boston, MA: Allyn & Bacon, 2006.

Periodicals

"Inmate Living Conditions," Inmate Services and Conditions of Custody in Saskatchewan Correctional Centres, October 2002. http://www.legassembly.sk.ca/officers/omb/Locked_Out/02%20Living%20Cond.pdf.

"Waiting to Die: The American Prison Experience," Prisoners' Voices, Prison Activist Resource Center, December 1, 2006. http://prisonactivist.org/?q=node/view/47.

Kenneth Anderson, "An American Gulag? Amnesty International Disgraces Itself," *Weekly Standard,* June 13, 2005.

Nathan Bierma, "Doing Time: Do Correctional Facilities Correct Anything?" *Books & Culture,* January/February 2004.

Alvin J. Bronstein, "Incarceration as a Failed Policy," *Corrections Today,* August 2005.

Bureau of Justice, "Criminal Offenders Statistics," November 13, 2005. www.ojp.usdoj.gov.

Jack Cowley, "Statement of Testimony: Commission on Safety and Abuse in America's Prisons," *Journal of Law & Policy,* April 19, 2005. http://law.wustl.edu/Journal/22/p187Cowley.pdf.

Jamie Fellner, "Prevalence and Policy: New Data on the Prevalence of Mental Illness in US Prisons," *Correctional Mental Health Report,* January 10, 2007.

Glenn A. Fine, "Statement Before the Commission on Safety and Abuse in America's Prisons," April 19, 2005. www.usdoj.gov.

Steve Heilig and David E. Smith, "Arresting the Jail Juggernaut: Drug Treatment Instead of Imprisonment," San Francisco Medical Society, 2005. www.sfms.org.

Peter Hitchens, "There Is a Way to Beat Crime—Fewer Human Rights, Tougher Prisons and Admitting that Nothing Deters Killers Like the Death Penalty." *Mail on Sunday,* March 30, 2003, p. 62.

Jim Holt, "Decarcerate?" *New York Times Magazine,* August 15, 2004.

Douglas Hurd, "Does Prison Really Work?" *Spectator,* May 14, 2005.

John Janda, "The Mind of the Parolee: A View from the Trenches," *Friends Committee on Legislation Newsletter,* August/September 2004. www.fclca.org.

Byron R. Johnson, "Religious Programs and Recidivism Among Former Inmates in Prison Fellowship Programs: A Long-Term Follow-Up Study," *Justice Quarterly* June 2004.

Edward I. Koch, "Harsh Punishments Curb Crime," *NewsMax,* April 28, 2005.

Barry Krisberg, "A Case Against Mass Incarceration," *Los Angeles Times,* January 18, 2005.

Chris Levister, "A Sweatshop Behind Bars," *WireTap Magazine*, September 13, 2006. http://www.wiretapmag.org/stories/41481.

Greg Mathis, "Alternative Sentencing Can Reduce Prison Population," *Call & Post*, May 12–18, 2005.

John McCain, "Torture's Terrible Toll," *Newsweek*, November 21, 2005.

Charles Murray, "Simple Justice," *Sunday Times* (London), January 25, 2004.

Vincent Schiraldi and Geri Silva, "Three Strikes: Law that Fails on All Counts," *Los Angeles Times,* March 7, 2004.

Susannah Sheffer, "Bearing witness to prison brutality," *Tikkun*, March–April, 2005.

Leslie Crocker Snyder, "Reform the Reforms," *New York Times*, January 8, 2006.

Lois Spear, "Reforming the System: Rehabilitation Needs a Chance," *America*, July 31, 2006.

Mary Zahn and Gina Barton, "Tougher Sentencing Law Carries Hefty Price," *JSOnline*, November 20, 2004. www.jsonline.com.

Web sites

Bureau of Justice Statistics (www.ojp.usdoj.gov/bjs). A government Web site with excellent statistical information about the death penalty in the United States. Contains numerous poll results, statistical analysis, and fact sheets about the death penalty, the executed, and those on death row.

Prison Activist Resource Center (http://prisonactivist.org). PARC is a prison abolitionist group committed to exposing and challenging the institutionalized racism of the prison industrial complex. Their Web site has article links and forums, and an interesting Prisoners' Voices section that contains testimonials written by inmates.

Prison Policy Initiative (http://www.prisonpolicy.org). This is a non-profit group that documents the impact of mass incarceration on individuals, communities, and the national welfare. Its Web site contains a wealth of information on prisons, including policy briefs, fact sheets, maps, and other information that is useful for reports.

Prison Talk (http://www.prisontalk.com). This Web site links to hundreds of forums where people discuss issues related to prisons, including recidivism, drug treatment, alternatives, prison violence, mandatory sentencing, and three-strikes laws.

Index

Picture Credits

Cover: photos.com
All photos © AP Images